A FUGITIVE PLANNER'S GUIDE TO EMPIRE

AGAPE
AGAINST GLOBAL APARTHEID & PLANETARY ECOCIDE

A FUGITIVE PLANNER'S GUIDE TO EMPIRE

AGAPE
AGAINST GLOBAL APARTHEID & PLANETARY ECOCIDE

solutionsforpostmodernliving.org

A Fugitive Planners Guide to Empire
First edition: June 20, 2025
© 2025, Muindi Fanuel Muindi
© 2025, solutionsforpostmodernliving

ISBN: 979-8-218-65861-8
Printed by solutionsforpostmodernliving

CONTENTS

Introduction 7

Empire & empires 10

The Makings of Maroon Infrastructures 38

The Racial Fracture 52

The Environmental Fracture 76

Between Force & Power 80

Confronting Our Traumas 110

Rape & Femicide 120

Empire's Next Moves & Maroon Countermeasures 126

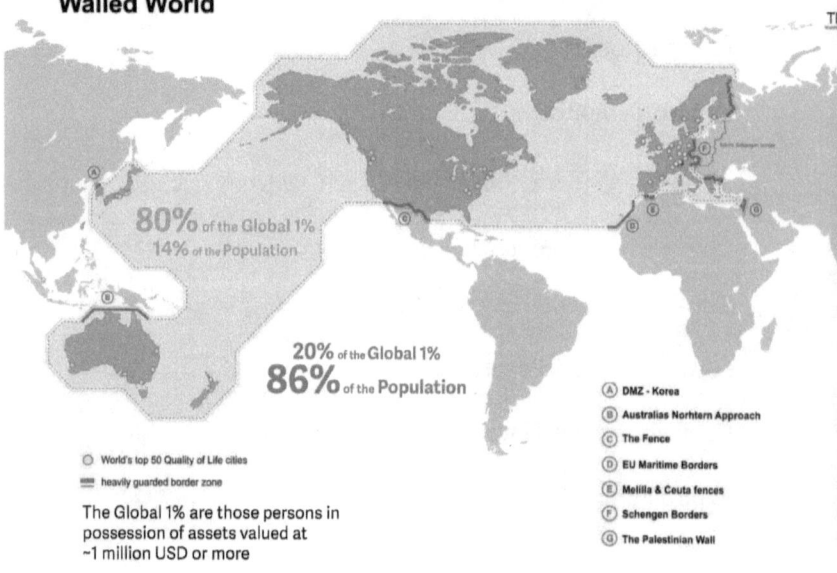

INTRODUCTION
Against Global Apartheid & Planetary Ecocide

For more than six millennia, the virus of patriarchal imperialism and its attendant maladies (war, conquest, enslavement, degradation, pollution) have been a greater or lesser scourge on our planet and her peoples.

Six centuries ago, however, new and more virulent strains of the virus emerged, turbocharged by racist and capitalist techniques and technologies of power. These new strains of patriarchal imperialism, aggravated by the unspeakable brutalities of capitalist war and racializing rule, have plunged our planet and her peoples into a social and ecological death spiral from which there may be no recovery.

Indeed, by all reliable accounts, we are fast approaching the terminal stages of this death spiral, the endgame of patriarchal imperialism and racial capitalism...

Ours is the Age of Global Apartheid and Planetary Ecocide.

It is an age marked by a dire deepening of the deathly double fracture that is the defining product of the fusion of patriarchal imperialism and racial capitalism: one fracture dividing the world between the "superior races" who dominate and devastate and the "inferior races" of the dominated and devastated; the other fracture dividing the world between the "civilized" realms where human culture prevails and the "environment" where wild and primitive natures cling to existence.

"Global Apartheid" names the regimes of murder by commission and omission, of organized abandonment and managed neglect, that maintain and advance the powers and privileges of the "superior races" and the "talented tenths" — the latter being those "exceptional specimens" of the "inferior races" who desperately vie to emulate and rival their "superiors" by violently distinguishing themselves from the "ordinary specimens" of their kind.

"Planetary Ecocide" names the "managed depletion" of the "environment" in the service of the pleasures and profits of the masters of the civilized realms of human culture — these masters being bent on maximizing the powers and privileges that they enjoy at the top of the aforementioned racial hierarchies.

Against this grim reality, the Against Global Apartheid and Planetary Ecocide (AGAPE) research group was convened to imagine and organize radical resistance. This text is a synthesis of AGAPE's inquiries so far.

Empire and empires

To grasp the global system of domination we inhabit today, it is essential to distinguish between empires (with a little 'e') and Empire (with a capital 'E').

Individual empires, such as those of Rome, Britain, or the United States, are discrete historical entities—political, military, and economic formations that wield power at particular times and places.

By contrast, Empire is the underlying system—a transhistorical logic of domination, exploitation, and control that transcends any single empire. Empire evolves by adapting to changing conditions, integrating regional systems of governance and intensifying patriarchal, racial, and capitalist hierarchies to sustain its authority.

Empire is not static. It has grown from fragmented, pre-modern patriarchal structures that were often localized and relatively "low-intensity," into an integrated global system that wields the unspeakable brutalities of capitalist war and racializing rule as accelerants of conquest and exploitation. This transformation defines the long centuries of domination that have shaped our world.

THE LONG SIXTEENTH CENTURY
Conquistador Capitalism: the Genoese-Iberian Crucible

The foundations of modern Empire were forged in the sixteenth century through the partnership between Genoese financiers and the Spanish and Portuguese empires. Genoese elites operated as the financial architects of a system that externalized nearly all costs—military protection, administration, and production—onto their Iberian allies. In return, Spain and Portugal extracted wealth and labor from colonized territories through enslavement, indenture, and dispossession, creating a machinery of extraction as brutal as it was systematic.

This collaboration was sanctified by dynastic alliances and the authority of the Catholic Church. The Genoese supplied the capital, Iberian aristocrats enforced extraction, and the Church provided spiritual justification. Together, they introduced two defining fractures of modern Empire: the racial stratification of humanity into "superior" and "inferior" breeds, and the reduction of nature to a reservoir of exploitable resources. These fractures became the backbone of a global system of domination.

Indigenous peoples and enslaved Africans bore the brunt of this new order. Their communities were shattered, their kinship networks severed, and their lives reorganized to serve imperial extraction. Once-thriving cultures, rooted in reciprocal relationships with the land, were fragmented into what Empire renders as "flesh"—bodies stripped of autonomy and relationality, reduced to instruments of labor.

Empire's domination extended beyond mere physical violence. Indigenous systems of kinship, consensus, and warfare were co-opted and weaponized. Rivalries among communities were exploited, and divisions were exacerbated to weaken resistance. Even leaders who sought to protect their people were often forced to act as intermediaries within the colonial apparatus. This redirection of resistance fractured opposition, embedding exploitation into the social fabric of colonized populations.

The Genoese-Iberian phase revealed the core logic of Empire: fragmenting life—social, cultural, and ecological—into extractable parts. By disassembling societies and reorganizing them into reservoirs of wealth and labor, Empire established a system of extractive and racializing rule that thrived on severed relationships, erased autonomy, and institutionalized inequality. This model, refined in the sixteenth century, became the template for the imperial expansion and capitalist domination that followed.

THE LONG SEVENTEENTH CENTURY
Mercantile Capitalism: the Dutch Innovation

The seventeenth century brought a critical transformation with the rise of Dutch hegemony and the innovations of the Dutch East India Company (VOC). Unlike the Genoese, who depended on aristocratic militaries, the VOC internalized protection costs, maintaining its own armed forces and merging financial and military power into a single corporate entity. This shift made protection a capital asset, extending the reach and efficiency of Empire.

This period also institutionalized state sovereignty through the Treaty of Westphalia (1648), which formalized a system of competing empires. While ostensibly designed to manage conflicts, the treaty preserved the overarching structure of Empire, integrating corporate executives and state administrators in a fusion of private profit and public power. The

VOC's innovations demonstrated how costs previously externalized could be repurposed to strengthen imperial domination.

In colonized societies, the VOC's approach was one of calculated disassembly. Communities were reorganized into coerced labor forces, stripped of autonomy and communal bonds, and transformed into production units for global markets. The VOC refined Empire's logic of fragmentation, further reducing people to commodified "flesh," their vitality extracted to sustain imperial operations.

Traditional governance systems, alliances, and militias were dismantled or absorbed into the VOC's private military. Indigenous rivalries were manipulated to fracture resistance, turning opposition into self-destruction. Land was seized and converted into plantations, uprooting Indigenous populations and severing their ties to ancestral territories. Enslavement, indenture, and forced cultivation produced commodities like spices and sugar for European consumption.

The VOC institutionalized exploitation with brutal efficiency. Colonized bodies were dehumanized, landscapes were reorganized, and wealth was funneled to the imperial core. By merging financial, military, and administrative power, the Dutch innovations deepened Empire's parasitic dynamic, creating a model of domination that would shape global capitalism for centuries.

THE LONG NINETEENTH CENTURY
Industrial Capitalism: British Consolidation

The nineteenth century marked a decisive evolution in Empire as Britain internalized production costs during the industrial revolution. Colonies were transformed into extraction zones, supplying raw materials for British factories and consuming finished industrial goods. This global supply chain entrenched racial and environmental hierarchies, with colonized peoples enduring exploitation while their lands were stripped of resources to fuel industrial expansion.

The Concert of Europe (1814–1914) stabilized this system, maintaining a balance of power among European empires while ensuring their collective dominance over colonized territories. British imperialists institutionalized wage labor, colonial governance, scientific racism, and national finance, consolidating a global capitalist order centered on Britain's factories and banks.

To sustain industrial capitalism, Empire restructured the metabolic systems of colonized societies. Traditional agriculture, which had nourished local populations and maintained ecological balance, was replaced by export-oriented monocultures. Subsistence crops gave way to commodities like sugarcane, tea, cotton, and rubber, leaving communities malnourished and dependent on imported food. Fertile soils were depleted, forests razed for plantations, and water systems diverted to irrigate industrial agriculture. These metabolic flows were forcibly redirected, channeling sustenance into Britain's factories and markets, leaving devastated lands and impoverished populations in their wake.

Empire thrived on fragmentation. Colonized bodies were reduced to laboring flesh even further, severed from kinship networks and reconstituted as tools of production. Their lands, drained of life, became extensions of Britain's industrial machinery. This fragmentation mirrored the exploitation of British workers, who toiled under similar systems of extraction and control. Domestic exploitation reinforced colonial domination, creating a symbiotic relationship that cemented Britain's industrial supremacy.

By reorganizing human and ecological systems, the industrial phase institutionalized extraction as a global norm. It severed regenerative and relational ties in favor of a system that thrived on dispossession and dependency.

THE LONG TWENTIETH CENTURY
Logistical Capitalism: U.S. Hegemony & the Formalization of Empire

The twentieth century marked the rise of the United States as the dominant force within Empire, introducing a transformative innovation: the internalization of transaction costs. U.S. hegemony restructured global capitalism around logistics, financial services, telecommunications, and digital infrastructure. Institutions like the IMF, World Bank, WTO, and SWIFT formalized this system, weaponizing global interdependence. By converting transaction liabilities into capital assets, multinational corporations gained unprecedented control over economic flows, consolidating Empire's dominance.

Unlike its German rivals—who, lacking an expansive overseas empire, pursued aggressive military expansion in Europe and were ultimately defeated in two world wars—the U.S. leveraged its settler-colonial empire to integrate North America and link the

Atlantic and Pacific Oceans. Historian Gareth Stedman Jones observes, "Historians who speak complacently of the absence of the [overseas imperialism] characteristic of European powers merely conceal the fact that the whole internal history of U.S. imperialism was one vast process of territorial seizure and occupation. The absence of territorialism 'abroad' was founded on an unprecedented territorialism 'at home.'"

After World War II, the U.S. absorbed the remnants of the Nazi German and Japanese empires, redefining Empire as a circulatory system centered on itself, sustained by ports, shipping lanes, transnational financial institutions, and, more recently, digital infrastructures. This system enabled the seamless movement of capital, goods, and labor between the Euro-Atlantic and Asia-Pacific while concealing the coercive foundations of global capitalism.

At the heart of U.S. hegemony was consumerism, which stabilized domestic populations by channeling dissent into the pursuit of goods and credit. Mass consumption, paired with financialization, optimized societies for productivity while reinforcing global racial hierarchies and accelerating ecological destruction. These dynamics yielded today's regime of Global Apartheid and Planetary Ecocide, where systemic inequality and environmental collapse are intertwined.

Empire's infrastructure expanded to uphold its extractive systems, particularly across the post- and neo-colonies of the Global South. Seaports, airports, pipelines, railways, and telecommunications networks were designed not to serve local needs but to expedite resource flows to the imperial core. This infrastructural violence facilitated widespread ecological devastation: forests razed, rivers dammed, and agricultural lands eroded, with colonized and dispossessed communities bearing the environmental burdens.

In the imperial core, impoverished migrants became the invisible machinery of logistical capitalism. Labor-intensive industries—agriculture, meatpacking, and sweatshop manufacturing—depended on their hyper-exploited labor. Displaced by imperial economic policies, they were commodified upon arrival, reduced to undervalued "flesh" essential to production yet systematically dehumanized within the circuits of capital.

More than reshaping global life, this phase entrenched Empire's domination so thoroughly that its machinery, omnipresent and deeply embedded, often seemed invisible. Under U.S. hegemony, Empire reached unprecedented levels of integration, its circulatory systems woven so seamlessly into daily life that they appeared natural, even inevitable. Beneath this veneer, however, lay the violent exploitation and ecological devastation that sustained them. The Global North reaped the benefits—consuming and profiting—while the Global South bore the costs: fragmented lives, ravaged ecosystems, and depleted resources.

"INTERNALIZATION"

Capitalism, at its core, is financial and parasitic in nature. Like a virus, it hijacks non-capitalist structures within host societies, draining them of vitality and often destroying them in the process. Historically, capitalism may have emerged multiple times, but it typically either killed its host or was itself killed by its host before it could fully entrench itself. The process of internalization, however, allowed capitalism to evolve into a more insidious form—sustaining its hosts in a zombie-like state and enabling the infection to spread further.

At each stage of its evolution, capitalism adapts by preserving, repurposing, and parasitizing critical systems to ensure its survival, even as it hollows out societies and ecosystems. In the Genoese phase (conquistador capitalism), it operated as a pure parasite, draining the Spanish Empire through financial manipulation and resource extraction. During the Dutch phase (mercantile capitalism), it co-opted the host's arms and defensive mechanisms, transforming them into tools that safeguarded and expanded its predatory reach. The British phase (industrial capitalism) seized the digestive systems of the host—production and consumption—fueling industrialization while metabolizing entire societies into engines of systemic transformation. By the U.S. phase (logistical capitalism), capitalism had refined and optimized the circulatory systems of its hosts—global commercial and monetary infrastructures—to consolidate planetary dominance and deepen its entrenchment within every ecological and social vein.

In its current phase, capitalism is mutating into surveillance capitalism, an even more invasive form that hijacks the sensory and nervous systems of its hosts. Through pervasive data capture, algorithmic control, and artificial intelligence (AI) platforms, it embeds itself into the most intimate dimensions of life. Human attention, perception, and emotional responses are captured, commodified, and manipulated, ensuring that social behaviors, desires, and imaginaries are aligned with the imperatives of capital accumulation. In this form, capitalism does not merely monitor and predict behavior; it shapes and engineers it, transforming individuals and societies into extensions of its logic.

Looking ahead, capitalism is showing clear signs of mutating further into biocapitalism, a form that internalizes and commodifies the costs of social and ecological reproduction. It hijacks the reproductive systems of its hosts, intensifying its parasitic grasp over life itself. While this trajectory appears novel, its roots extend deep into earlier forms of racialized and gendered exploitation. During the transatlantic slave trade, enslaved populations were subjected to brutal reproductive regimes, forced to maximize labor output while minimizing the costs of their own social and biological reproduction. Today, these dynamics re-emerge under neoliberal regimes of so-called innovation, where human reproduction, care work, and ecological regeneration are increasingly framed as marketized resources. This logic subjects life-making processes to systems of surveillance, commodification, and control, deepening inequality under the pretext of efficiency and sustainability.

Yet this trajectory is far from linear. Capitalism has always experimented along multiple axes, testing and refining strategies for survival and expansion. Historical moments, such as the transatlantic slave trade's attempts to internalize reproductive costs, demonstrate that these strategies often operate in parallel, rather than sequentially. Under specific conditions, one approach achieves dominance, and the empires that master it ascend to hegemonic status within Empire. It is this adaptive, opportunistic nature—capitalism's ability to parasitize, mutate, and entrench itself—that ensures its persistence, even as it corrodes the very societies, ecosystems, and bodies upon which it relies for survival.

This ongoing process of mutation reveals capitalism not merely as an economic system, but as a planetary contagion—parasitic, self-replicating, and increasingly invasive—requiring ever-new territories, forms of life, and systems to consume. Its survival depends on its ability to move deeper into the social, ecological, and biological realms, transforming living systems into extractable, commodified flows. In doing so, capitalism brings its hosts ever closer to exhaustion, setting the stage for crises that simultaneously mark its limits and the potential for its unraveling.

THE PRESENT: SHIFTING HEGEMONIES
Surveillance Capitalism and Challenges to Euro-Atlantic Hegemony

Today, Empire is in crisis, fractured by shifting centers of power. The rise of China as an economic and military force challenges long-dominant Euro-Atlantic hegemony, yet this ascent does not signal a break from Empire but a reconfiguration of its analytics. China's ruling elite has appropriated and adapted the tools of racial capitalism and patriarchal control developed by Euro-Atlantic powers, forging a new iteration of imperialist racial capitalist patriarchy.

China's trajectory follows a familiar pattern in which regional powers assimilate and weaponize Empire's structures to assert dominance. In the late 19th century, Japan pursued a similar course, modernizing through the selective adoption of Euro-Atlantic technologies of domination. As Mark Driscoll notes in *Absolute Erotic, Absolute Grotesque: The Living, Dead, and Undead in Japan's Imperialism, 1895-1945* (2010), Japanese elites inoculated themselves with the "toxicity" of European racial capitalism, deploying its extractive logics to defend sovereignty while asserting regional power. China's modernization follows this blueprint, leveraging capitalist systems and technologies while maintaining a centralized, Han-centric nationalist framework. It internalizes the costs of labor reproduction, resource extraction, and infrastructural expansion—endeavoring to pioneer a new form of capitalism that hijacks the reproductive systems of its hosts—while positioning itself as a global competitor to the United States. This escalating rivalry deepens Empire's fractures, intensifying extractive pressures on Indigenous lands, ecosystems, and bodies, and fueling a neo-Scramble for Africa under the guise of development.

The current crisis of Empire arises from China's resurgence after centuries of subjugation under Euro-Atlantic dominance. While the U.S. successfully integrated smaller East Asian client states—Japan and the jewels of its erstwhile empire, South Korea and Taiwan—into its global capitalist system on terms favorable to U.S. hegemony, it faces a more existential challenge with China: a territorially vast, militarily independent nation encompassing nearly a fifth of the world's population. The U.S. had attempted to incorporate China as "the world's factory," extracting surplus value from its labor force while circumventing the racial and political anxieties tied to mass migration. Containerized logistics, just-in-time production, and extraterritorial Special Economic Zones—reminiscent of 19th-century treaty port concessions—were central to this strategy. Yet this gambit, rooted in racist assumptions forged during the 19th-century coolie trade, opium wars, and scramble for treaty port concessions, has backfired. China not only absorbed the mechanisms of global capitalism but also leveraged them to emerge as a formidable rival, shifting economic gravity from the Euro-Atlantic to the Asia-Pacific.

Pursuing hegemony, China is building an alternative logistics and surveillance infrastructure to rival the U.S.-dominated system. This strateigy has two key components. First, through the Belt and Road Initiative (BRI), China is reshaping global trade and resource flows by integrating Africa, Asia, the Middle East, and Latin America into a China-centered network of railways, roads, ports, and pipelines. Second, it is developing a digital "stack" of surveillance platforms, telecommunications networks, cloud services, and AI technologies to reduce dependence on and surpass U.S. technological dominance

However, China cannot pursue hegemony through direct military confrontation with the U.S. or the outright destruction of U.S.-centered infrastructure. Instead, by subversively working within this infrastructure, it positions itself as a partner to nations disillusioned with U.S. imperialism. Through strategic investments in physical and digital infrastructures, China presents an alternative path to development that appears less reliant on military coercion. AI-driven platforms, data-sharing agreements, and technology transfers have become key tools in this strategy, enhancing its influence over emerging technological ecosystems. Many nations in the Global South welcome this approach, viewing Chinese investment as a counterbalance to U.S. dominance. Yet they increasingly find themselves caught in cycles of debt dependency and new forms of exploitation under Chinese-led projects.

Recognizing China's ambitions, the U.S. has intensified efforts to destabilize key regions where China is making inroads. By fostering economic and political crises, the U.S. seeks to disrupt China's initiatives, forcing it to expend resources on stabilizing partner nations. This includes undermining pro-China regimes through political coups, proxy conflicts, and opposition movements. Instability near major Chinese infrastructure projects—ports, railways, pipelines—creates operational risks, compelling China or its trusted allies (such as Russia) to intervene diplomatically or militarily. The U.S. also pressures potential partners to avoid deep integration with Chinese networks through sanctions, diplomatic isolation, and military maneuvers.

As this rivalry escalates, regions critical to China's BRI—particularly in Africa, Southeast Asia, and the Middle East—become contested zones. China faces a strategic dilemma: overcommit resources and risk overextension, or remain passive and see its investments and credibility erode. Meanwhile, the U.S. exploits these vulnerabilities by engineering disorder, a long-standing imperial tactic of forcing rivals to exhaust themselves in stabilizing contested territories.

Under the Trump administration, the U.S. has emerged as the leading architect of global destabilization. Its erratic foreign policy—marked by unilateralism, trade wars, and hostility to multilateral institutions—has spread uncertainty worldwide. This unpredictability serves a strategic purpose: a chaotic world disrupts China's ability to build a competing infrastructure, forcing it to divert resources toward crisis management. By obstructing China's initiatives, the U.S. maintains its dominance within Empire's infrastructure of control.

This strategy is rooted in the structural advantage of an established hegemon. The U.S., as the center of the global system, does not need to innovate or overhaul its infrastructure to maintain control. It is easier to undermine a rival system than to build one. Historically, dominant powers have leveraged this advantage to destabilize challengers rather than adapt themselves. Upstart powers, in contrast, must innovate to displace incumbents. If they succeed and defend their innovations, they often rise to global leadership. But established hegemons, aware of this dynamic, use their centrality to sow disorder and sabotage these efforts before they take root, often co-opting them once the threat is neutralized.

U.S. foreign policy reflects this calculated destabilization. Rather than reforming the global system, it seeks to prevent China from creating a parallel network of influence. By provoking crises in regions where China has invested heavily, the U.S. aims to sabotage infrastructure projects and undermine China's credibility. As Empire mutates through this phase of crisis and competition, the balance of power will depend on which nation can more effectively leverage instability to its own advantage.

And yet, none of this dismantles Empire's extractive and exploitative logic—it merely reshapes and reinforces it. The global order remains anchored in domination, inequality, and systemic extraction, even as hegemonies shift. Empire's infrastructure mutates, its technologies are repurposed, and its fractures deepen, but its foundational imperatives—accumulation, control, and extraction—endure. Hegemonic rivalry does not mark the end of Empire; it accelerates its destructive momentum, extending its parasitic reach into new frontiers and onto new hosts.

The Diffusion of Racial Capitalist Patriarchy

At the heart of Empire's evolution lies its capacity to transform and diffuse patriarchal systems on a global scale. Pre-modern patriarchies, often localized and relational, were magnified and repurposed by Empire through racial capitalist logics, colonial technologies, and modern bureaucracies, creating expansive architectures of domination. This process relied on alliances with regional patriarchal elites, who localized Empire's tools while maintaining their dominance.

China's rise, like Japan's Meiji-era modernization, exemplifies this hybridization. Both nations adopted Empire's industrial and technocratic systems, blending them with existing patriarchal and nationalist hierarchies to assert regional power. In India, the ascent of upper-caste Hindu nationalism reflects a similar fusion: modern capitalist governance intertwines with pre-modern caste, religious, and gendered systems to reinforce Brahmanical supremacy while aligning labor and reproduction with capitalist imperatives. These examples show how regional powers not only adapt to but also contribute to Empire's evolving system of control, perpetuating domination while reinforcing global inequality.

Empire's strength lies in its parasitic adaptability—mutating through co-production with regional elites who sustain localized hierarchies while reproducing global domination. This hybridization consolidates patriarchal systems, weaponizing them to extract value and deepen gendered, racialized, and ecological fractures. Far from monolithic, Empire operates as an interconnected constellation of regimes, where pre-existing inequalities are scaled up, modernized, and embedded into planetary systems of exploitation.

The Enduring Fractures of Empire

As the current hegemon faces challenges, some suggest the possibility of a multi-polar world where multiple regional powers share influence. While this might redistribute power among individual empires (e.g., a Han-supremacist China, a Hindu-supremacist and caste-stratified India, a white-supremacist Europe and North America, the Arab-supremacist petrostates of the Persian Gulf), it does not necessarily dismantle Empire's foundational logic. Instead, such multi-polarity risks producing a meta-stable Empire in which rival powers, despite their competition, collaborate to sustain the fractures of racialized domination and ecological exploitation under new arrangements.

Empire thrives on both continuity and transformation, adapting to power shifts while preserving its core logic of extraction, hierarchy, and control. Its fractures—between humanity and nature, and between so-called "superior" and "inferior" races—remain the bedrock of its dominion. From the Genoese-Iberian alliance to the ascendance of China, Empire's history is one of relentless adaptation and expansion, ensuring its survival across centuries.

The Desertion of Empire

The fractures of Empire—between peoples, and between humanity and nature—are not incidental byproducts but its very foundations. Sustained by a system that extracts, divides, and exploits under the guise of progress, stability, and order, Empire's logic perpetuates domination. Yet, these same fractures expose its vulnerability. The accelerating crises of ecological collapse, racialized inequality, and geopolitical conflict reveal the fragility of a system that perpetually and purposefully breaks its promises.

To be an anti-imperialist today is to recognize that neither the consolidation of current hegemonies nor the rise of new ones offers a solution. Whether led by NATO's neoliberal globalists or the emergent BRICS coalition (Brazil, Russia, India, China, South Africa), Empire's logic remains rooted in domination—genocidal, ethnocidal, and ecocidal. A multi-polar order is not the antithesis of Empire but a variation of its machinery, ensuring its fractures persist under shifting arrangements of power.

The task, then, is not to steer Empire away from its trajectory of self-destruction but to desert it altogether. To desert Empire is not a retreat into nihilism; it is an active refusal to perpetuate its violence and embrace the transformative potential in its unraveling. This involves deconstructing the administrative statements, technical implements, built environments, and dramatic elements that sustain

Empire's logic while (re)constructing alternatives that nurture autonomy and conviviality.

Petit & Grand Marronage

The desertion of Empire unfolds as a continuum of refusals and (re)creations, encompassing practices of petit and grand marronage. Rooted in the Black radical tradition, marronage embodies a spectrum of escape and resistance that deconstructs systems of domination while reconstructing autonomy and conviviality.

Petit marronage, aligned with what Fred Moten and Stefano Harney term the "general antagonism," consists of everyday acts of defiance—small, incremental refusals that chip away at systems of exploitation. These include reclaiming time from labor, creating temporary autonomous zones, and subtly subverting oppressive ideologies. Such acts mirror the fluid, dispersed nature of pack formations—small, dynamic groups that evade and disrupt the constraints of larger, hierarchical systems.

Grand marronage, by contrast, represents a radical rupture—a collective and decisive refusal of Empire's logic through flight and autonomy, reaching its apogee in the "general strike." Historically, it manifested as enslaved peoples fleeing plantations to establish maroon communities or, in the most profound acts, leaping en masse from slave ships to escape the horrors of bondage. Grand marronage is not merely physical escape but a spiritual and existential leap toward freedom, often at the cost of life. Like the transformative force of mass movements, it embodies collective rupture and creates the space for new forms of sociality to emerge.

Together, petit and grand marronage form a "tidalectic" of resistance. Incremental acts of petit marronage lay the groundwork for grand gestures of refusal, while the audacity and vision of grand marronage inspire and amplify the quieter, everyday acts of defiance. This interplay offers a dynamic framework for dismantling Empire and imagining life beyond its reach.

Maroon Infrastructures

What would it mean to build infrastructures that enable forms of petit and grand marronage today, that heighten the general antagonism and create the material conditions of possibility for a general strike? How might we design autonomous spaces and systems of survival that sustain incremental acts of defiance while also preparing for collective flight and radical transformation?

Such infrastructures would need to balance practicality with subversion, combining the adaptability of pack formations with the transformative energy of mass movements. Thriving in the margins of Empire, they would rely on this flexibility to evade control while fostering resilience and solidarity. Just as maroon societies flourished in spaces Empire deemed "uninhabitable," modern maroon infrastructures could carve out possibilities for autonomy and conviviality within the fractures of its decline.

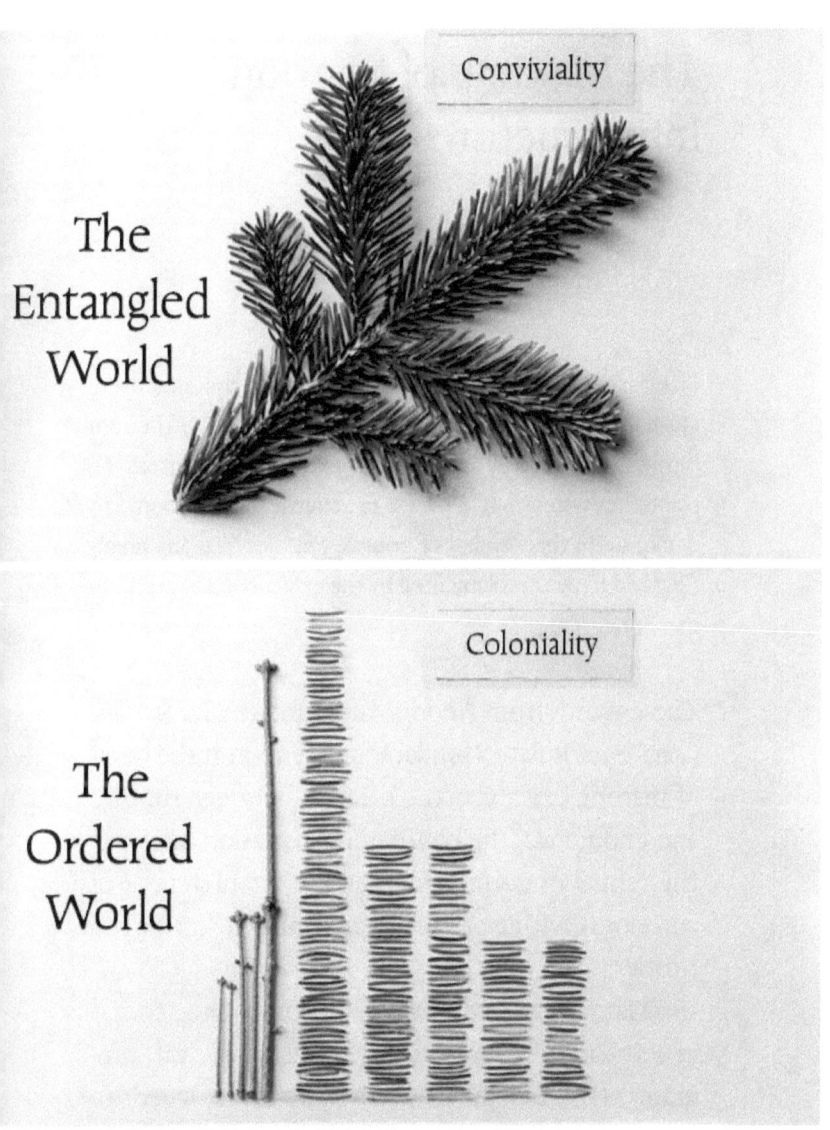

The Entangled World — Conviviality

The Ordered World — Coloniality

The Makings of Maroon Infrastructures

"[Histories of marronage] point to the ongoing conundrum entailed in moving from confinement to freedom. The flight from captivity was not only an attempt to extricate oneself from the plantation system but a means to unsettle its hegemony, to demonstrate the viability of possible outsides. Yet, any unsettling had to be complemented by the exigencies and practicalities of resettling."

These words from AbdouMaliq Simone's *The Surround* (2022) encapsulate a fundamental tension at the heart of maroon existence: the paradox between rupture and endurance, the continuous oscillation between the refusal of domination and the establishment of autonomy within or in close proximity to hostile territories.

Maroon infrastructures—encompassing counter-territories, counter-logistics, and survival programs—are living, adaptive systems designed to resist the coercive order of Empire and create the conditions for its planetary abolition. Through complex, improvisational, and relational networks, these infrastructures unsettle the techno-political machinery of control, creating zones of refuge, survival, and insurgent regeneration.

Rather than static havens, maroon infrastructures evolve as dynamic ecosystems thriving through polyrhythmic practices of care, negotiation, and mutual adaptation. These networks, shaped by the cumulative knowledge of generations resisting oppression, do not merely negate existing systems of control but continuously prototype new forms of relational autonomy. This text imagines the making of maroon infrastructures as a world-making practice characterized by four interwoven dimensions: (Administrative) Statements, (Technical) Implements, (Built) Environments, and (Dramatic) Elements. Each dimension plays a vital role in sustaining maroon life amidst conditions of domination and ecological precarity.

These dimensions, rooted in both material and symbolic practices, illustrate how maroon communities cultivate autonomy under ever-shifting pressures of repression and resource scarcity. To conceptualize these dimensions, the analogy of a communal meal serves as a useful reference point

Statements: Methods and Measures

Administrative statements provide the methods and measures necessary for organizing maroon life. These are not rigid, top-down directives; rather, they function like recipes, outlining both procedural steps (methods) and proportional requirements (measures) needed to sustain collective well-being.

For example, in the preparation of a meal, a recipe articulates the proper methods (e.g., chop, sauté, simmer) and appropriate measures (e.g., precise or flexible ingredient quantities) to enable a satisfying result. Similarly, maroon administrative statements take the form of negotiated protocols, truces, mutual aid agreements, and resource-sharing guidelines that serve as recipes to sustain cooperation without coercion.

These statements emphasize adaptability and improvisation. Citing Fred Moten and Stefano Harney in *The Undercommons* (2018), we might say that they embody fugitive planning as a militant form of preservation, safeguarding difference and autonomy while rejecting the rigid bureaucratic policies characteristic of modern state structures. In maroon infrastructures, these statements might function as adaptable blueprints for resource allocation, seasonal planting cycles, or strategies for conflict resolution. Like recipes, they encourage those who take them up to modify and supplement them to fit local and seasonal needs, preferences, resources, and conditions—adjusting for taste, dietary restrictions, and the available ingredients, cookware, and appliances.

This improvisatory approach aligns with Pierre Clastres' (1974) theory of "societies against the state," where leadership is subordinated to communal needs and power is diffused to prevent its consolidation into oppressive authority. Through these flexible yet coherent frameworks, maroon communities are able to maintain autonomy and relational accountability across time and shifting conditions.

Implements: Tools and Techniques

Implements are the material tools and techniques that enable maroon communities to meet their practical needs. These tools are essential for survival, defense, mobility, and ecological stewardship, evolving in response to fluctuating environmental and social conditions.

Continuing the meal analogy, implements include both cooking tools (e.g., pots, pans, stoves, measuring cups) and eating tools (e.g., plates, bowls, serving spoons). Techniques for handling these implements—such as sautéing or portioning—illustrate the intimate connection between material resources and embodied practices.

In maroon contexts, implements encompass navigation tools, self-defense weapons, and ecological knowledge systems essential for foraging, farming, and concealment. Harriet Tubman's renowned success on the Underground Railroad, for instance, was rooted in techniques for reading environmental cues—river crossings, forest paths, and celestial navigation. Similarly, maroon communities across the Americas developed specialized tools and practices, including dugout canoes in coastal Georgia, tree hollows for concealment, and coded signals, all of which supported life on the margins of colonial control.

Environments: Places and Pathways

Built environments refer to the physical and spatial infrastructures that support maroon autonomy by providing refuge, mobility, and sites for communal assembly. These environments decentralize power by fostering interconnected networks of relational spaces designed to evade surveillance and maintain self-governance.

Consider the various spaces associated with a meal: the kitchen where food is prepared, the dining area where it is consumed, and the pathways connecting these spaces. In maroon life, built environments perform analogous functions. Hidden paths, fortified settlements, and communal gathering grounds form a dispersed yet cohesive network of relational autonomy.

Examples include the intricate networks of quilombos in Brazil, which utilized dense forests and rugged landscapes to create impenetrable sanctuaries. These environments served as both physical refuges and experimental arenas for alternative social organization, enabling maroon communities to rehearse ways of living beyond the constraints of colonial law. Simone's concept of the surround captures this spatial strategy, emphasizing environments that remain "slightly out of joint"—visible yet elusive, fostering both rest and regeneration.

ELEMENTS: ACTORS AND FACTORS

Dramatic elements encompass the actors and situational factors that shape the unfolding dynamics of maroon life. These include both the individuals who assume various leadership roles—organizers, caretakers, defenders, cherished animal, vegetal and mineral allies—and the contextual forces influencing their actions.

In the context of a meal, the dramatis personae include cooks, servers, diners, and bussers, while dramatic circumstances might involve seasonal changes, economic instability, or the emotional states of those involved, all of which can affect the meal's ingredients, cost, ease of preparation, and the enjoyment of those who partake. Similarly, in maroon infrastructures, actors navigate shifting conditions through relational accountability, employing skill and trust to maintain communal stability. Their roles are shaped by the interplay between internal needs and external pressures, such as state repression, ecological challenges, and social conflict. These actors embody the resilience and adaptability that are essential to maroon praxis.

Maroon Infrastructures in Practice

Maroon infrastructures, both historical and contemporary, exemplify the resilience and adaptability of strategies that challenge Empire's control over space, bodies, and resources. These infrastructures do not merely react to oppressive systems but actively prefigure new, relational ways of organizing life, care, and resistance. Across the Black Atlantic, the experiences of fugitivity—from the establishment of territorial sanctuaries to complex logistical networks—demonstrate how the flight from captivity laid the foundations for autonomous worlds structured by mutual care and accountability.

COUNTER-TERRITORIES:
Quilombos and Maroon Settlements

Quilombos, such as the legendary Palmares in Brazil, are quintessential examples of maroon counter-territories. These communities harnessed the landscape's natural defenses—dense forests, rugged hills, and remote swampy regions—not merely as barriers against colonial incursions but as environments conducive to reimagining social and political life. The Great Dismal Swamp in the southeastern United States similarly sheltered maroon settlements, using its vast and difficult terrain to protect communities from capture. In both contexts, the terrain became a medium through which fugitives could evade surveillance and fortify their autonomy.

As Clóvis Moura (1981) emphasizes, quilombos were not merely refuges but centers of ongoing political and social resistance. By destabilizing plantation economies and ideologies of racial domination, these settlements enacted what Moura calls a "radical negation" of slavery's foundational logics . Their refusal to subordinate themselves to colonial authority required military campaigns to uproot, underscoring their existential threat to the plantation system.

Moreover, maroon communities often employed diplomacy to sustain their autonomy. Negotiated truces with colonial authorities or neighboring Indigenous groups were tactical maneuvers, not concessions. These agreements enabled maroons to maintain their networks of care, mobility, and defense while minimizing direct confrontation . In this way, maroon counter-territories balanced concealment with visibility, retreat with strategic negotiation.

COUNTER-LOGISTICS:
The Underground Railroad and Black Star Line

Mobility and secrecy are essential components of maroon resistance, forming the basis of counter-logistical infrastructures that outmaneuver the surveillance and control mechanisms of the state. The Underground Railroad exemplified such an infrastructure, with a vast network of secret routes, safe houses, and alliances across abolitionist communities . Fugitives and conductors relied on human and environmental resources to facilitate escape, from coded communication systems to deep ecological knowledge. Harriet Tubman's mastery of these logistical elements—including celestial navigation and knowledge of river crossings—enabled her to guide dozens of fugitives to safety.

The Underground Railroad's success relied on the interplay of administrative statements (e.g., maps), technical implements (e.g., hidden compartments in carriages), built environments (e.g., river crossings, land routes, iron forges, foundries, waterways, and other natural or human-made hiding places), and dramatic elements (e.g., fluctuating weather conditions, shifting patrol patterns). These networks continually adapted to external pressures, demonstrating the flexibility essential for sustaining maroon mobility.

Similarly, Marcus Garvey's Black Star Line sought to disrupt colonial control over global trade and transportation by creating an independent shipping network for African-descended people . Though eventually sabotaged by state interference and internal divisions, the Black Star Line represented a broader diasporic vision of autonomy. By attempting to reclaim maritime infrastructure, it challenged the racialized economic systems that had long governed the movement of goods and people across oceans.

Both the Underground Railroad and the Black Star Line illustrate how counter-logistics function as a crucial dimension of maroon praxis, ensuring that fugitivity remains a viable strategy under conditions of state repression. Through adaptive logistical infrastructures, maroon communities navigate and undermine dominant networks of power.

Survival Programs
The Black Panther Party and Community Care

Survival programs extend maroon infrastructures into the realm of community care and social reproduction. The Black Panther Party's initiatives—ranging from free breakfast programs for children to community health clinics and copwatching patrols—challenged the state's monopolization of welfare and security. These programs aimed to provide both material and emotional resources, ensuring that Black communities could survive and thrive despite systemic neglect .

Administrative statements played a central role in formalizing these efforts. Protocols for resource allocation, volunteer coordination, and food distribution exemplified the meticulous planning necessary to sustain such programs. For example, the Party's breakfast programs involved carefully designed measures to procure, prepare, and serve meals to large numbers of children, ensuring both nutritional adequacy and communal participation .

Technical implements such as supply chains, kitchen equipment, and medical tools supported the programs' practical functions, while dramatic elements—including the Party's visible presence through uniforms and public patrols—served to deter violence and mobilize solidarity. However, as Simone's The Surround highlights, this visibility also heightened vulnerability to counterinsurgency, illustrating the precarious balance between public assertion and concealment .

COMPLEMENTARY PRACTICES:
Clandestine Noncompliance & Belonging to the Surround

The complementary practices of clandestine noncompliance and relational belonging are essential to maroon infrastructures. Clandestine noncompliance involves tactics of misdirection, invisibility, and tactical deception designed to subvert surveillance and capture. Afro-Brazilian Capoeira's concept of malícia—a form of embodied tactical agility—provides a striking example of how physical movement can serve as both a survival strategy and a mode of defiance.

In contrast, belonging to the surround emphasizes the cultivation of mutual care and adaptive trust. This relational practice operates through what Simone describes as "intensive contiguity," where peripheral spaces and networks become central to survival and resistance. Marginal environments—abandoned buildings, urban underpasses, and secluded pathways—offer maroon communities opportunities to rehearse new forms of relational autonomy without falling prey to the full capture of state power.

The Surround as Infrastructural Effect

The surround, as conceptualized by Simone, encapsulates the dynamic process through which maroon infrastructures unsettle and reconfigure dominant systems of control. These infrastructural effects manifest in spaces and practices that operate "slightly out of joint," creating zones where insurgent futures can be rehearsed. Through cycles of disruption, evasion, and care, maroon infrastructures transform survival into a generative praxis of liberation, resisting co-optation by state and capitalist systems.

By integrating counter-territories, counter-logistics, and survival programs, and by embracing the ineffability of clandestine noncompliance and the opacity of the surround, maroon infrastructures reveal the transformative power of relational autonomy. They challenge Empire's foundational logics, creating possibilities for alternative worlds where survival itself becomes an act of radical freedom and resistance.

The Racial Fracture

Denise Ferreira da Silva's *Toward a Global Idea of Race* (2007) and *Unpayable Debt* (2022) illuminate how the "analytics of raciality" operates through three deeply entangled dimensions: demography, geography, and history. These dimensions form a global framework for organizing human populations into racial hierarchies, assigning distinct identities to specific spaces and temporalities while linking them to narratives of development, civilization, and progress. This framework defines the first of Empire's double fractures: the racial fracture.

Empire constructs race as a system of psychosexual, sociocultural, and geopolitical hierarchies, with Blackness occupying the abject position as a universal signifier of defectiveness. The analytics of raciality sustains this order by codifying techniques of domination through demographic classification, geographic partitioning, and historiographic sequencing. Together, these dimensions "naturalize" the subjugation of non-white populations and "justify" their perpetual administration and control.

Demography
Determining Race

The dimension of demography in the analytics of raciality establishes racial categories—white, Black, red, brown, yellow—as seemingly universal and immutable markers of identity. These categories are far from neutral descriptors; they are constructs imbued with hierarchical value, positioning whiteness as the zenith or centerpiece of humanity and all other racial identities as lower or eccentric deviations. Blackness, in particular, is consistently cast as the most abject and deficient, associated with psychosexual, sociocultural, and geopolitical defects that are presumed to emanate from a subhuman biological essence.

This hierarchical racial taxonomy is central to the global project of Empire. It informs the recognition, governance, and subjugation of populations within political, economic, and social systems. Blackness is constructed as the prototypical "problem" in these systems, embodying everything that whiteness is not: primitiveness, irrationality, criminality, and lack of progress.

The Myth of Racial Progress: The Race Relations Cycle

The liberal globalist myth of racial progress—articulated most explicitly by early 20th-century American sociologists through the "race relations cycle"—provides a framework for managing and ostensibly resolving racial differences. This cycle, described as "progressive and irreversible," maps a trajectory from racial conflict to accommodation, assimilation, and ultimately amalgamation (miscegenation). It is a teleological narrative that assumes nonwhite groups must gradually abandon their "primitive" cultural traits, adopt the "civilized" culture of whiteness, and merge into the racial hierarchy through interracial unions.

However, as Denise Ferreira da Silva argues in *Toward a Global Idea of Race*, the race relations cycle is designed to fail when applied to Black populations. Blackness, unlike other racialized identities, is framed as an insurmountable barrier to full inclusion. Sociologist Robert E. Park, for instance, attributed this failure not to cultural differences but to physical traits, arguing that "the chief obstacle to the assimilation of the Negro" lay in the enduring visibility of Blackness. This visibility—encoded in phenotypic markers—renders Black bodies permanently estranged within the white-dominant world, regardless of their cultural or social adoption of whiteness.

The Role of Blackness in Racial Hierarchy

Blackness holds a unique and foundational position in the global racial order, functioning not merely as one among many racial identities but as the ultimate signifier of abjection against which all others are measured. Whiteness is constructed through its absolute opposition to Blackness, while other racialized groups are positioned along a spectrum based on their relative proximity to or distance from Blackness.

This dynamic entrenches anti-Blackness as a global phenomenon, enduring even in contexts where whiteness is no longer the dominant power. While non-Black groups may assert that they have equaled or surpassed whiteness, Black people and Blackness remain fixed as universal symbols of "the primitive," "the slave," and "the criminal." These associations shape the governance and perception of all other racial identities. For example, even within liberal globalism's multicultural narratives, Blackness is still denigrated, cast as a failure to assimilate, modernize, or adapt.

Racial hierarchies have occasionally conferred "honorary white" or "model minority" status on certain groups—such as the broad categorization of East Asians in apartheid South Africa or the specific designation of Japanese people as "honorary

Aryans" in Nazi Germany. However, within these systems, Blackness and whiteness are constructed as immutable and opposing categories. Blackness, as a collective identity, is categorically excluded from "honorary white" and "model minority" status because the analytics of raciality position Blackness as the negation of whiteness—Blackness is equated with primitiveness, while whiteness is synonymous with civilization. While exceptional Black individuals from the so-called "talented tenth" may occasionally be granted a form of "honorary white" recognition, this distinction is framed as their personal transcendence of Blackness rather than as a redefinition or elevation of the Black race as a whole.

The persistent association of Blackness with "the primitive" legitimizes its perpetual management and control. Historically, enslavement was framed as the mechanism through which Blackness was introduced to "civilization," serving as a model for subsequent systems of governance. This logic continues to operate today, manifesting in institutions like the prison-industrial complex, which treat Black populations as objects of control, experimentation, and administration

DEMOGRAPHY AS A FRAMEWORK OF CONTROL

The analytics of demography extend beyond classification; they serve as a framework for governing and exploiting racialized populations. The hierarchies established through demography inform techniques of surveillance, labor extraction, and social control. Blackness is rendered a problem to be solved, whether through forced assimilation, containment, or elimination.

The logic of racial demography ensures that the racial hierarchy is reproduced across generations. Blackness is systematically excluded from the category of full humanity, framed as a defect that must be corrected through proximity to whiteness or erased through processes of miscegenation or eradication. Meanwhile, whiteness remains the unmarked standard, universal and invisible, against which all other identities are measured.

GEOGRAPHY:
Spatializing Race

The second dimension of the analytics of raciality, geography, maps racial categories onto specific regions, producing a racialized cartography of the world. Whiteness is aligned with Europe and the West, Blackness with Sub-Saharan Africa, redness with the Americas, brownness with South Asia, and yellowness with East Asia. Transitional regions—such as Southeast Asia, Central Asia, West Asia, North Africa, and parts of Southern and Eastern Europe—are marked by hybrid categorizations. This spatial organization enforces a logic of racial difference that links identity to land, naturalizing racial distinctions as inherent, fixed, and immutable.

However, as Denise Ferreira da Silva's work reveals, this spatialization is not monolithic; it adapts to regional histories and contexts, reflecting the flexibility of Empire's racial logic. The geographic codification of race takes on distinct forms in places like the United States and Brazil, demonstrating how racial hierarchies are shaped and reinforced differently based on local climates, economies, and colonial histories. While both regions perpetuate anti-Blackness and racial stratification, their mechanisms for doing so differ in ways that illuminate the broader operations of geography within the analytics of raciality.

THE UNITED STATES: DISCRETE CATEGORIES OF BELONGING

In the United States, racial geography is structured around rigid binaries that position Blackness and whiteness as fundamentally irreconcilable. Blackness is linked to enslavement, criminality, and subhumanity, while whiteness is idealized as the pure, unblemished standard of humanity. This binary sustains a racial hierarchy that obsessively polices the boundaries of whiteness, stigmatizing any perceived mixture with Blackness. The infamous "one-drop rule" institutionalized this ideology, perpetuating the notion that even the slightest trace of Black ancestry irrevocably marked a person as Black, making Blackness an inescapable and indelible identity.

By contrast, Native American ancestry is governed by the logic of blood quantum, which functions in the opposite direction. While one drop of Black ancestry permanently assigns an individual to Blackness, Native ancestry is imagined to dissolve into whiteness over generations through intermixture. Blood quantum thresholds for tribal belonging frame Native identity as something that diminishes with each successive generation, aligning with the settler-colonial goal of Indigenous erasure. Blackness, on the other hand, is constructed as an enduring stain that persists across generations, an unyielding mark of exclusion from whiteness.

These contrasting logics reveal the distinct mechanisms of racial domination in the settler-colonial project. Blackness is rigidly contained, perpetuated, stigmatized, and perversely fetishized as a threat to the purity of whiteness. Native identity is systematically eroded to fulfill the settler aim of eliminating Indigenous presence. Native blood is framed as a fleeting impurity that whiteness can absorb, while Black blood is treated as a contaminant that forever excludes individuals from the privileges of whiteness.

All other racialized groups are positioned in a precarious space between the Black and the Native, where proximity to whiteness confers a degree of social acceptability. It is more desirable to be seen as akin to the Native, who is imagined as assimilable, than to the Black, who is marked as perpetually outside the bounds of inclusion.

The spatial implications of this racial coding are profound. Whiteness is aligned with the temperate climates and perceived resemblance between North American and European landscapes, symbolizing spaces of civility, order, and governance. In contrast, Blackness, an import from the "uncivilizable" tropics, is relegated to spaces of captivity, exclusion, and labor exploitation. The spatial logic of the United States relies on rigidly fortifying divisions between spaces of whiteness and Blackness, upholding a vision of racial purity through systems of segregation and exclusion. This dynamic ensures that whiteness remains dominant and unchallenged, while Blackness is persistently marginalized, stigmatized, and confined to the periphery.

Brazil: Alloyed Whiteness in the Tropics

In Brazil, the geography of race operates through a different lens, emphasizing the logic of miscegenation and fluid gradations of racial identity rather than the rigid binary categories prevalent in the United States. As Denise Ferreira da Silva observes, Brazilian racism is anchored in the concept of "alloyed" whiteness, where whiteness derives strength and value through the calculated admixture of non-white ancestry. Unlike the American fixation on racial purity, Brazilian whiteness is constructed as adaptable and resilient, strategically fortified by miscegenation to endure the perceived challenges of the tropical environment.

This framework treats miscegenation not as a threat but as a mechanism for incorporating and ultimately erasing Blackness within a hierarchical racial order. Blackness is framed as an excess or defect to be gradually diminished through intergenerational mixing, producing "alloyed" whites deemed better suited to Brazil's climate. The celebrated "career" of Africans in Brazil, as Silva describes, is defined not by empowerment but by disappearance—a process through which phenotypic markers of Blackness are systematically erased over generations, ensuring whiteness's dominance while rendering Blackness increasingly invisible.

In Brazil, the ultimate ideal is not pure whiteness but rather a tempered and fortified whiteness. Blackness, however, is stigmatized as the most volatile and disruptive element to combine with whiteness, capable of producing profound psychosexual, sociocultural, and geopolitical "defects," even in small amounts. Despite this, Blackness is paradoxically viewed as a useful element to alloy with whiteness when handled in controlled and minimal doses. Other racialized groups are considered less volatile and easier to assimilate, with Indigenous Brazilians occupying the opposite end of the spectrum from Black Africans. Much like in the United States, where Indigenous identity is constructed as less threatening and more assimilable, Indigenous Brazilians are seen as the least disruptive element, facilitating the production of an "acceptable" alloyed whiteness within the Brazilian racial hierarchy.

Geography and the Global Logic of Racialization

Both the United States and Brazil exemplify how geography is used to naturalize racial hierarchies, but their differing approaches are part and parcel of a broader, overarching global logic. As Silva notes, the degree to which whiteness is valued in its "pure" or "alloyed" form depends on geography and climate. In temperate regions purported to resemble Europe, like North America, purity is privileged; in tropical regions purported to be hostile to European ways of life, like Brazil, admixture becomes a strategy for sustaining dominance.

This adaptability allows the analytics of raciality to maintain the underlying racial hierarchy across diverse contexts. Whether enforced through rigid segregation or subtle gradation, the spatial logic of Empire's racializing rule ensures whiteness remains central and dominant, while Blackness is persistently marginalized and denigrated. Regions deemed entirely unsuitable for European settlement, such as parts of Central Africa, are often constructed as spaces of "primitive" subcultures. These spaces, perceived as suffering from the absence of whiteness, are still portrayed as imitating and distorting whiteness from a distance—"aping" and "corrupting" white ideals in a manner that reinforces the view of Blackness as the antithesis of modernity, civilization, and progress.

The Geography of Anti-Blackness

Anti-Blackness, as Silva argues, is a persistent and defining feature of this racial geography, shaping how spaces are valued, governed, and utilized. In both Brazil and the United States, Blackness is relegated to spaces of exploitation and containment, such as the plantation, the American ghetto, the Brazilian favela, or the prison. These spaces are critical to the operations of Empire's racializing rule, functioning as laboratories for developing and refining techniques of control, extraction, and subjugation.

The global map of racialized spaces underscores the deeply interconnected dimensions of geography and demography. Blackness is consistently associated with Africa and the "primitive," while whiteness is linked to Europe and the "civilized." European expatriate enclaves, irrespective of their location, are constructed as symbols of order and progress, while Black neighborhoods outside Africa—whether in Europe, the Americas, or elsewhere—are stigmatized as sites of danger, degradation, and disorder. Globally, landscapes deemed desirable for settlement are marketed to European audiences as spaces of opportunity and prosperity, while poor Black African migrants are corralled into regions considered hazardous or toxic, reinforcing their exclusion from spaces of privilege and their confinement to zones of exploitation.

This spatialization does more than delineate where racialized bodies are permitted to exist; it "naturalizes" the unequal distribution of opportunity and resources. It "legitimizes" the expropriation of land and labor, framing such acts as necessary for progress. Colonial and postcolonial enterprises consistently portray themselves as benevolent missions to civilize or improve territories and populations deemed backward, unproductive, or threatening. Geography, in this context, serves as a mechanism for justifying domination: desirable spaces are reserved for whiteness and those proximal to it, while undesirable spaces are relegated to containment, marginalization, and extraction, particularly for Blackness and those furthest from whiteness. This dynamic not only sustains racial hierarchies but embeds them into the very landscapes and infrastructures that define the modern world.

GLOBAL APARTHEID

Expanding this logic to global geopolitics, the international apartheid regime, solidified under United States hegemony, uses nationality as a proxy for race, reproducing the racial hierarchies entrenched within the hegemonic nation's borders. Indigenous peoples without recognized nation-states are excluded entirely from this global racial order, rendered invisible and expendable within the frameworks of the global economy. Nations predominantly inhabited by those categorized as belonging to the "Negro" race—such as Black Africans and the most impoverished Caribbean populations, with Haiti serving as a stark example—are positioned at the very bottom, perpetually framed as zones of racial and economic deficiency.

Above the nations of Black Africa and the Caribbean in this global racial hierarchy are the so-called "coolie" nations of Asia, particularly India and China, whose populations were racialized during the era of slave emancipation as a labor force considered more "dependable" than free Africans. Competing alongside Asians are the settler-colonial nations of Latin America, whose populations, largely composed of "alloyed whites" and visibly mixed-race groups such as mestizos, pardos, and mulattos, are disparaged by white Europeans and North Americans for their supposed "racial impurities" and "deficient racial hygiene."

Meanwhile, Eastern Europe, Western Asia, Southern Europe, and Northern Africa are cast as liminal zones, transitional spaces between the white European race and the racialized populations of Sub-Saharan Africa and South and East Asia. These regions occupy an ambiguous place within the hierarchy, simultaneously othered and partially assimilated into whiteness, their populations framed as intermediaries between the fully included and the fully excluded.

This global racial hierarchy marginalizes Black nations to the furthest periphery, systematically excluding them from meaningful roles in shaping the international order. It justifies interventions into the lives and lands of non-white populations under the guise of "civilizing missions," often reframed as peacekeeping operations, development programs, or humanitarian aid. These narratives not only reinforce racial hierarchies but also embed them deeply within the international institutions that define the modern global system.

Geography and the Analytics of Raciality

The geographic dimension of Empire's racializing rule does more than assign races to specific regions; it produces and sustains racial hierarchies by framing certain spaces as inherently superior or inferior. Africa is imagined as a land of ungovernable Blackness, perpetually in need of external administration. Europe, by contrast, is positioned as the seat of rationality and governance, radiating progress outward to the rest of the world.

This spatial logic reinforces the other dimensions of Empire's racializing rule—demography and history—creating a comprehensive system for organizing human populations into hierarchical orders. The entanglement of geography with racial identity ensures that racial hierarchies are inscribed into the land itself, perpetuating systems of domination long after formal colonial rule has ended. As Silva's work demonstrates, geography is not simply the backdrop for racial hierarchies; it is an active participant in their construction and perpetuation.

History:
Temporalizing Race

The historical dimension of Empire's racializing rule weaves together the analytics of race and space by embedding temporal hierarchies into racialized identities. This framework constructs a linear timeline of progress that positions whiteness as the spearhead of modernity while relegating Blackness to the perpetual margins of primitiveness. Africa, central to this logic, is simultaneously cast as the origin of humanity and excluded from the trajectory of civilization, framed as stagnant and pre-modern.

Africa as the "Primitive" Origin

Africa holds a foundational role in the temporal logic of coloniality, positioned as the "dark continent," frozen in time and outside the trajectory of historical progress until colonization ostensibly "rescued" it by introducing it to history. Framed as the epitome of primitive life, Africa is depicted as perpetually awaiting salvation through external intervention. This narrative has long been employed to justify colonial conquest, enslavement, and resource extraction, rebranded in contemporary times as peacekeeping, humanitarian aid, and development. Such interventions are far from altruistic; they function as mechanisms to sustain Africa as a space of social death, perpetually subjected to external control and oversight.

International institutions extend the dynamics of domestic anti-Blackness onto the global stage. Across Africa, peacekeeping forces and philanthropic organizations wield unchecked authority, echoing the impunity with which police and civil administrations operate in Black communities across the United States. Africa, the most heavily patrolled region by peacekeeping forces, is subjected to this militarized paternalism under the guise of humanitarianism. Both systems collaborate to sustain Africa's depiction as a site of primitive failure, rationalizing its ongoing subjugation through the rhetoric of progress and benevolence.

By contrast, Asia is often depicted as home to age-old civilizations whose "genius" transferred westward to feed Western European modernity. China, India, and the Muslim world are acknowledged for their historical contributions but are framed as having stagnated at a crucial juncture, allowing the West to cross the finish line first and become the embodiment of universal progress. Africa, by contrast, is denied even this recognition of historical depth, reduced instead to a timeless void awaiting salvation.

This dual narrative reflects coloniality's strategy of erasure and appropriation. Africa is exploited as a raw resource materially and symbolically, while Asia's cultural and intellectual heritage is co-opted to affirm Western dominance. These narratives are not inherent truths but imposed constructions designed to justify global hierarchies.

CONTRASTING TEMPORALITIES: THE RACE RELATIONS CYCLE

The race relations cycle, a liberal globalist framework for racial progress, underscores the temporal dimension of Empire's racializing rule. It imagines a progression from conflict to accommodation, assimilation, and finally amalgamation (miscegenation). While ostensibly universal, the cycle systematically excludes Black populations, particularly in Africa and its diaspora. In the United States, Blackness is marked by rigid binaries, with the infamous "one-drop rule" ensuring permanent exclusion from whiteness. Africa, in this schema, is the ultimate repository of failure, reinforcing Blackness as incompatible with progress.

In Brazil, the cycle adopts a different temporality. Blackness is not rigidly excluded but diluted through miscegenation, imagined as a process of whitening over generations. This logic treats Blackness as a defect to be erased, aligning with Brazil's narrative of racial democracy while maintaining white dominance. Despite these regional differences, both frameworks converge in their treatment of Africa as a site of stagnation, justifying ongoing interventions that perpetuate the continent's dependency.

Temporal Logic of Enslavement and Control

Enslavement exemplifies the historical mechanism through which Blackness is introduced to "civilization." This logic persists in contemporary institutions such as the prison-industrial complex, development projects, and international border regimes. Africa is framed as the prototype of failure, perpetually requiring external governance. Its nations, many labeled "failed" or "fragile," are treated as wards of an international order, Empire, that positions itself as the arbiter of civilization.

This framing extends to Black diasporic populations, who are subjected to the same logics of control. Migrants from Africa, fleeing poverty and instability, are profiled as "illegal immigrants" in wealthier nations, confined to zones of exploitation and subjected to heightened surveillance. These border regimes, as Silva argues, use nationality as a proxy for race, ensuring that Blackness is criminalized and excluded from full participation in global mobility and modernity.

Africa and Global Apartheid

The global racial order enforces a form of apartheid that marginalizes Africa and its diasporic populations. Militarized border regimes and bureaucratic immigration systems function as modern-day "pass laws," preserving the privileges of wealthier, whiter nations while restricting the movement of migrants from the Darker Nations. Africa's citizens endure the harshest restrictions, their exclusion reinforcing the continent's role as a supplier of resources and labor rather than a participant in "progress."

Black Africans who gain limited access to the wealthier core nations of Empire are often funneled into low-wage labor markets, or forced to undervalue their labor despite possessing extensive experience and credentials for higher-wage sectors. In these spaces their contributions are systematically exploited while their humanity is devalued. This dynamic reflects Africa's broader positioning within the global order as a site of extraction and control, where its worth is measured solely by its utility in sustaining the prosperity of others.

FROM ORDERED WORLD TO ENTANGLED WORLD

Denise Ferreira da Silva's work compels us to confront and dismantle the "Ordered World" — the colonial world sustained by the analytics of raciality. This world naturalizes demographic determinability, geographic separability, and historiographic sequentiality, embedding and entrenching racial hierarchies in the techniques, infrastructures, and logics of policing, bordering, and governance. At its core, this order systematically excludes Blackness, and all those proximal to it, from full humanity, perpetuating domination and exploitation under the guise of progress and civility.

Silva challenges us not only to abolish the techniques of this order, but also to deconstruct the epistemologies and ontologies that sustain it. She exposes how systems of control and violence are legitimized by fixed identities, bounded spaces, and linear narratives of development. By deconstructing this Ordered World, Silva envisions the possibility of an "Entangled World" — one characterized by demographic indeterminacy, geographic non-locality, and historiographic non-eventuality, which collectively foster an ethic of mutuality, care, and relationality.

DEMOGRAPHIC INDETERMINACY: This condition rejects rigid, hierarchical racial, ethnic, and cultural classifications. Demographic indeterminacy counters the colonial logic that uses fixed categories to dictate value, inclusion, and governance. Instead, it embraces the opacity, multiplicity, and confluence of identities, unmooring populations from rigid markers of difference that have historically justified domination.

GEOGRAPHIC NON-LOCALITY: Geographic non-locality disrupts the colonial spatial logic that ties identity to bounded, segmented territories. It rejects the idea that certain people inherently "belong" to specific places, challenging systems of inclusion, exclusion, and dispossession. In the Entangled World, space is reimagined as relational, porous, and entangled, resisting the territorial fixity that reinforces control and exclusion.

HISTORIOGRAPHIC NON-EVENTUALITY: This departure from linear, teleological history challenges the notion of universal developmental stages through which all peoples are expected to progress. Historiographic non-eventuality opposes the colonial narrative of "progress," proposing instead a revolutionary, relational, non-causal and non-hierarchical understanding of time. It allows diverse temporalities to coexist, to influence one another, and to merge into confluences, refusing subordination to a single, Eurocentric timeline of advancement.

In the ENTANGLED WORLD, race no longer determines value or belonging, space is no longer carved into zones of inclusion and exclusion, and history no longer serves as a measure of developmental "success." Silva's vision challenges us to construct maroon infrastructures that enable beings, places, and temporalities to co-exist and resist the colonial impulse to impose order and control.

The Environmental Fracture

Empire's power rests on a dual fracture: the division between so-called inferior and superior races, examined in the previous chapter, and the division between humanity and nature, which we now turn to. These fractures uphold its hierarchies, enabling planetary-scale extraction and perpetuating ecological devastation. The technosphere—the artificial, human-dominated subsystem of Earth—not only emerges from these fractures but also deepens them, embedding Empire's logic of domination into the planet's very systems.

Built on violence and dispossession, the technosphere subordinates Earth's lithosphere, hydrosphere, atmosphere, and biosphere to its extractive machinery. It enacts ecocide on a planetary scale while intensifying racialized inequalities. Its expansion has required the systematic suppression of Transformative Ecological Knowledge (TEK)—relational, adaptive practices that have sustained more-than-human worlds for millennia.

Rooted in mutuality and regeneration, TEK embodies a legacy of ecological care and balance.

Empire, dismissing these practices as "primitive," displaced and destroyed them while selectively extracting their insights for imperial gain. This calculated erasure paved the way for the Anthropocene, a geologic epoch defined by cascading ecological crises—all driven by Empire's unrelenting techno-political machinery.

THE LATE VICTORIAN HOLOCAUSTS
The Catastrophe of TEK's Destruction

The Late Victorian Holocausts stand as a grim testament to the catastrophic consequences of erasing TEK. Between 1870 and 1914, three waves of drought and famine—exacerbated by the El Niño Southern Oscillation—claimed the lives of over 30 million people across tropical Africa, Asia, and South America. These deaths were not inevitable outcomes of climatic conditions, but the result of colonial policies that systematically dismantled Indigenous systems of ecological resilience and reoriented resources to serve imperial greed.

In India, British colonial authorities commodified and emptied communal grain storage systems, which had historically buffered communities against famine. They redirected local food supplies to imperial markets, prioritizing exports over survival, and imposed monocultural cash crops that degraded soil and undermined agricultural diversity. Railroads, heralded as symbols of progress, facilitated the extraction of wealth rather than the equitable distribution of sustenance. Millions starved along these tracks, as grain flowed out of famine-stricken regions to fuel imperial profits. As Mike Davis highlights in *Late Victorian Holocausts* (2000), "Millions died, not outside the 'modern world system,' but in the very process of being forcibly incorporated into its economic and political structures."

The systemic violence of these policies resonates with Friedrich Engels's observation in *The Condition of the Working Class in England* (1845):

"When one individual inflicts bodily injury upon another such that death results, we call his deed murder. But when society places hundreds [...] in such a position that they inevitably meet a too early and an unnatural death, one which is quite as much a death by violence as that by the sword or bullet; when it deprives thousands of the necessaries of life, places them under conditions in which they cannot live — forces them, through the strong arm of the law, to remain in such conditions until that death ensues which is the inevitable consequence — knows that these thousands of victims must perish, and yet permits these conditions to remain, its deed is murder just as surely as the deed of the single individual."

The ethnocidal erasure of TEK epitomizes this "disguised, malicious murder." Practices of communal resource sharing, conservation, and redistribution—rooted in generations of relational ecological wisdom—were violently suppressed and replaced with imperial systems of extraction. Stripped of these adaptive practices, colonized populations were rendered defenseless against environmental crises, their survival contingent on exploitative colonial infrastructures that prioritized profit over human life.

The Late Victorian Holocausts reveal the dual logic of Empire: racialized exploitation and ecological devastation. By dismantling TEK, colonial powers intensified vulnerability to famine and ecological collapse, enabling the violent incorporation of colonized regions into the technosphere of imperial racial capitalism. Engels's words underscore the nature of this violence, which, though sanitized by legal and systemic structures, remains murder nonetheless. Its legacy persists in the ongoing fragility imposed upon communities stripped of their ecological autonomy—a fragility that continues to echo in our age of escalating climate crises and dispossession.

The Late Davosian Holocausts
Ethnocide in the Neocolonial Present

The destruction of TEK persists today in what can be called the Late Davosian Holocausts—a series of crises shaped by climate catastrophe, extractivist development, and the white savior industrial complex. These crises, much like the Late Victorian Holocausts, are not natural inevitabilities but systemic outcomes of exploitation and mismanagement.

Since 2000, climate-driven disasters have claimed millions of lives globally through malnutrition, floods, disease, and extreme heat. By mid-century, projections estimate hundreds of thousands of additional deaths annually, escalating to tens of millions by the century's end. The continued burning of fossil fuels alone, through air pollution, is expected to prematurely claim over 100 million lives if current trends persist and bring the planet from 1.5 degrees of warming up to two degrees. These staggering figures reveal not only the direct impact of climate change but also the compounding effects of systemic neglect, exploitation, and the relentless prioritization of extraction over life.

Development aid, often framed as a solution, entrenches dependency and perpetuates extraction. Under the guise of relief, it reinforces systems of managed depletion, stabilizing crises to maintain global hierarchies while eroding local autonomy.

The white savior industrial complex further suppresses TEK, displacing communal resilience with systems that prioritize markets over care. This logic mirrors the colonial infrastructures of the past, channeling resources toward imperial centers while leaving vulnerable communities to bear the brunt of environmental and social collapse.

The Late Davosian Holocausts exemplify the violence of Empire's logic: a slow erosion of life through extractive systems that prioritize profit over well-being. Addressing this ongoing ethnocide demands more than technical solutions. It requires the decomposition of the technosphere: dismantling the structures of extraction, honoring TEK, and embracing a regenerative ethic rooted in care, confluence, and rhythm. Only then can the fractures of Empire begin to heal, and life move toward a future beyond its destructive reach.

Maroon Infrastructures as TEK

To desert Empire is to reclaim and (re-)create TEK. Maroon infrastructures, rooted in the fugitive practices of Maroons and Indigenous peoples, serve as dynamic frameworks for resisting domination and nurturing regeneration. These infrastructures transform what Empire deems "inhospitable," "impassable," and "unruly" natures into allies. In our time of escalating climate catastrophes, extractivist development, and the managed depletions perpetuated by the white savior industrial complex, these unruly and inhospitable forces are no longer distant abstractions; they are central to rethinking how we live, resist, and repair. As the Earth liberates itself from Empire's confines through storms, floods, and fires, it invites us to align with its disruptive power and seek new ways of flourishing.

RECOGNITION: Empire dismisses unruly natures—forests, swamps, floods, pests—as obstacles to progress or threats to order. Maroon infrastructures invert this logic, recognizing these forces as critical allies. Just as fugitive communities once sought refuge in the Great Dismal Swamp, embracing what colonizers called "unmanageable" wilderness, today's Maroon infrastructures ally with the disruptive agency of nature. In Octavia Butler's *Wild Seed* (1980), Anyanwu's town, hidden in plain sight amidst the forest, exemplifies this ethos: "They were in the middle of her town, surrounded by villages. No European would have recognized a town, however, since most of the time there were no dwellings in sight. [...] The villages of the towns were well organized, often long-established, but they were more a part of the land they occupied, less of an intrusion upon it." Maroon infrastructures strive to inhabit the world as part of its flows, rather than as an imposition upon them.

RECOLLECTION: Reclaiming TEK is not a return to the past but a transformation of ancestral practices to meet the demands of the present. Communal grain storage, polycultural farming, and regenerative land use once shielded communities from environmental crises. Maroon infrastructures recollect these practices, adapting them for modern struggles against extractive economies and ecological collapse. These efforts do not merely sustain life; they challenge Empire's false dichotomies between humanity and nature, teaching us to live as participants in more-than-human systems of care.

RESISTANCE: Empire's infrastructures—railroads, dams, pipelines, and planetary modelling and monitoring systems—are designed to extract, fragment, and control. Maroon infrastructures disrupt this logic, transforming tools of domination into instruments of resistance and subversion. Railroads built to transport wealth from the periphery to the imperial core can instead convey climate refugees and carry goods and information that sustain fugitive communities. Digital technologies, reclaimed from surveillance capitalism, can serve as tools for anonymity, mutual aid, and confluence. Resistance within Maroon infrastructures is not reactive but creative, building the systems necessary for life beyond Empire.

REPAIR: As Empire's extractive violence devastates ecosystems and communities, repair emerges as both an ethical imperative and a revolutionary act. Maroon infrastructures prioritize repair not as a return to an idealized past, but as a practice of (re-)creation—an ongoing process of forming new, reciprocal relationships with human and non-human worlds. This approach aligns with the art of yobitsugi or "joint-calling," a practice of repair that gathers fragments from different wholes to create something entirely new. Here, repair is not about restoring a previous state but embracing the openness of reassembly, accepting that what is mended remains fragile, susceptible to future fractures, yet worthy of care nevertheless. The resilience lies in the act of repair itself, not in the permanence of the product.

Maroon infrastructures embody this ethos of creolizing repair. They revive degraded soils from monoculture farming, redirect watersheds altered for industrial use, and rebuild social bonds fractured by colonialism and capitalism. These acts are less about preservation and more about transformation, forging connections that sustain life while welcoming the inevitability of change.

As Derek Walcott wrote of Antillean art: "Break a vase, and the love that reassembles the fragments is stronger than that love which took its symmetry for granted when it was whole." Maroon infrastructures reflect this love in their restoration of fragmented histories and ecologies, creating new wholes from disparate, ill-fitting pieces. Through these acts of repair, they cultivate conditions for resilience and regeneration, embracing life's fragility while nurturing its infinite capacity to begin again.

THE ANATOMY OF MAROON INFRASTRUCTURES

Maroon infrastructures are pathways to desert Empire and nurture an Entangled World. Grounded in TEK and the fugitive practices of Maroons and Indigenous peoples, they decompose the technosphere and foster planetary flourishing. Maroon infrastructures enable recognition, recollection, resistance, and repair, rejecting Empire's rigid hierarchies and extractive boundaries. They also cultivate demographic indeterminacy, geographic non-locality, and historiographic non-eventuality, weaving these principles into the foundations of regeneration.

STATEMENTS: METHODS AND MEASURES

Empire governs through metrics that impose control and extraction. It divides populations into "useful" and "wasteful," ecologies into "productive" and "unproductive," stabilizing its hierarchies through the language of measurement. Census systems reinforce rigid racial categories to allocate resources unequally, while agricultural surveys are biased towards plantation monocultures, reducing otherwise cultivated lands to either "wastelands" or reserves.

Maroon infrastructures dismantle these frameworks and construct measures rooted in demographic indeterminacy. These measures value relationships and confluences over fixed classifications. Instead of rigid racial or ecological categories, fugitive plans focus on shared responsibilities and overlapping roles that sustain collective well-being.

For example, a fugitive measure might assess the extent and intensity of confluences rather than enforce exclusionary categories. Agroforestry practices that blend cultivated and wild landscapes illustrate this ethic, creating ecosystems that resist Empire's false dichotomies. These plans foster confluences, aligning methods with the rhythms of life and rejecting domination.

Implements: Tools and Techniques

Colonial tools—surveying instruments, extraction machinery, and monoculture technologies—enforce rigid boundaries and domination over landscapes. Empire's implements carve ecosystems into exploitable units, suppressing their natural dynamics.

Maroon infrastructures de-/re-construct these implements, transforming them into tools of connection and adaptability. Guided by demographic indeterminacy and geographic non-locality, Maroon tools hybridize identities and dissolve territorial fixity, fostering dynamic and confluential relations. Countersurveillance, for example, repurposes mapping technologies to support ecological migrations and human movement in ways that evade surveillance and control. Agroecological techniques like companion planting and seed-sharing networks create overlaps between cultivated and wild areas, fostering adaptive systems that sustain life.

Maroon tools collaborate with the land, embracing its rhythms and dynamics. They reject Empire's obsession with control, prioritizing care, (re-)creation, and resilience in their design and use.

Environments: Places and Pathways

Colonial infrastructures fragment and dominate landscapes. Dams displace communities while redirecting rivers for extraction; railways funnel resources to imperial centers; urban grids enforce rigid separations between human and non-human life.

These built environments impose static boundaries, reinforcing Empire's control.

Maroon infrastructures dissolve these divisions, creating environments that embody geographic non-locality and foster mobility, refuge, and regeneration. These spaces adapt to ecological and social shifts, offering sanctuary to both human and non-human life.

For example, a contested wetland might become a shared sanctuary, where displaced communities and migratory species find refuge. Informal pathways—used by foraging animals and climate migrants—can be transformed into connective corridors that sustain movement and collaboration.

Where Empire enforces separation—different places for different people and different purposes—Maroon infrastructures embrace entangled uses. They transform fragmented landscapes into dynamic confluences, enabling life to thrive through connection and adaptability.

Elements: Actors and Factors

Empire deploys engineers, bureaucrats, and soldiers as agents of control, wielding tools like data surveillance and disaster relief to enforce its binary logic of progress and backwardness. These agents impose rigid order, casting nature as blind chaos or untamed wilderness to be subdued.

Maroon infrastructures center actors who embody historiographic non-eventuality, rejecting the linear narrative of progress. Healers, storytellers, and growers emerge as entangled agents of transformation, shaping practices that reflect relational temporalities. Rather than suppressing natural forces, they engage with them as collaborators.

For Maroons, events that Empire labels as "natural disasters"—storms, droughts, and floods—often serve as opportunities for escape and renewal. Colonizers view these disruptions as setbacks to progress and catastrophes to control, but Maroon infrastructures see them as potential catalysts for co-adaptation and resilience.

For instance, a wildfire may regenerate soils and clear pathways for new growth, enabling both human and ecological recovery. These dramatic elements reframe upheaval as possibility, aligning human action with the rhythms of a dynamic, more-than-human world.

Unruly Futures

Maroon infrastructures guide us toward an Entangled World by weaving demographic indeterminacy, geographic non-locality, and historiographic non-eventuality into every aspect of life. They dismantle Empire's rigid hierarchies, transforming tools of domination into instruments of care, (re-)creating static environments as adaptive sanctuaries, and replacing agents of control with collaborators in resilience and renewal.

In our age of escalating climate crises and extractive destruction, Maroon infrastructures ally with the Earth's unruliness. They embrace storms, floods, and fires as collaborators that defy containment, transforming rupture into resurgence and insurgency. When rivers overflow imperial boundaries or wildfires reclaim monocultured fields, they clear pathways for regeneration and liberation. Our task is not to rebuild Empire's extractive systems but to join in the Earth's resurgence and insurgency, crafting infrastructures that nurture life amidst upheaval.

In Octavia Butler's Wild Seed, Anyanwu's community exemplifies how humans can exist as "more a part of the land [they] occupy, less of an intrusion upon it." Maroon infrastructures extend this vision, aligning with unruly and inhospitable natures to affirm a future beyond Empire's control—a future rooted in care, confluence, and conviviality for all beings.

The Anthropocene demands not mitigation within Empire's frameworks but a profound transformation—a radical (re-)creating of relationships between humans and the more-than-human world.

Transformative Ecological Knowledge (TEK) offers a guide for this (re-)creating. TEK is not a relic but a living, adaptive force, capable of fostering systems that thrive on mutuality and regeneration.

By reclaiming TEK and building Maroon infrastructures, we can decompose the technosphere and repair the fractures that sustain Empire. In deserting its logic of domination, we move toward an Entangled World—one where relationality, reciprocity, and care replace extraction and control.

Between Force & Power

Once, there was a conqueror who ruled through unmatched strength. His armies were vast, his weapons terrifying, and his victories swift. Wherever he marched, he made his intentions clear: submit or be destroyed. The people he conquered bowed—not out of reverence, but out of fear of the sword. His empire grew rapidly, built on the ruins of the defeated and held together by the ever-present threat of his might.

But dominance built on force alone is precarious. Over time, the conqueror found himself surrounded by whispers of rebellion. Though his victories had been absolute, they were fleeting. Each crushed uprising was soon followed by another. The cycle of conflict drained his coffers, stretched his armies, and bred resentment among the conquered. The conqueror began to see the cracks in his dominion: force alone could not hold it together. Dominance gained through strength would always demand more strength, leaving him both exhausted and vulnerable.

Then came the councilor, a cunning advisor who offered a new strategy. "Victory need not be fought for every time," she said. "Instead of crushing the defeated, make them enforce your rule themselves. Build laws that bind them. Write stories that glorify you. Make the world forget there was ever a time before your reign."

The conqueror listened and began to change his tactics. After his next victory, he did not burn the enemy's city to the ground. Instead, he summoned their leaders and declared a law: anyone who sought to trade, worship, or even travel would need his permission. This was the first rule, and to enforce it, he built a council—not of his soldiers, but of the defeated people themselves. They became the gatekeepers of his will, ensuring no one could act without his approval.

At first, the people resisted. They traded in secret and traveled through hidden paths. But the conqueror anticipated this and stationed watchmen at key crossings, punishing violators publicly. "See how the law protects order?" he proclaimed, masking his control as necessity. Exhausted by resistance and fearful of reprisal, the people complied—not out of agreement, but out of resignation.

Satisfied with this initial success, the conqueror turned to the councilor again. "The law binds them, but they obey only because they fear what I can do," he said. "What happens when they think I am no longer watching?"

"Then they must come to believe the law is theirs," the councilor replied.

So, the conqueror commissioned a grand history. Scribes wrote of his strength, his wisdom, and how his laws had brought peace and prosperity. "Before the conqueror," the stories claimed, "there was chaos. It was he who saved us." These tales spread far and wide, told by elders to children, sung by bards in the squares. Over generations, the people began to forget they had ever lived differently.

Years passed, and the conqueror's empire flourished—not because his armies marched, but because his rules had become systems. Judges enforced his laws. Priests praised his vision. Merchants followed his trade routes. The conqueror himself rarely needed to intervene. The people policed themselves, enforcing his dominance without his presence.

"This is the beauty of systems," the councilor told him. "You have built a machine that runs itself. Your strength is no longer conspicuous because it is omnipresent. Even those who never saw your sword now follow your rules."

But the councilor offered a warning: "This power depends on belief. If the people cease to trust the stories—if they see the chains for what they are—the system will falter. And when it falters, you will need your armies again."

The conqueror dismissed the warning, confident in his invincibility. Yet, beyond his borders, whispers of rebellion grew louder. In hidden valleys and dense forests, fugitive planners assembled in community. They shared memories of life before the conqueror's rule, passed down by the oldest among them. They told stories of a time when people walked freely, traded openly, and made their own laws.

The fugitive planners refused to live within the conqueror's system, choosing instead to (re-)create alternatives grounded in care and confluence. Their assemblies grew steadily in strength, number, and purpose, invisible to the conqueror's watchmen. When they rose against the empire, they did not confront its armies in open battle. Instead, they dismantled its systems piece by piece—chipping away from the outside while infiltrating and sabotaging from within. Through these acts, they exposed the coercion concealed beneath the empire's laws, revealing the fragility of its seemingly invincible order.

From Story to Theory

The tale of the conqueror reveals the interplay between force and power, exposing the mechanisms by which dominance is maintained and extended. Force, defined by its raw and immediate application, secures victories through direct confrontation and violence. Yet it is finite—exhaustive, unstable, and contingent. Each act of domination demands renewed effort, leaving the victor perpetually vulnerable to resistance. Power, by contrast, transcends the moment of victory. It transforms the outcomes of force into systems and structures that perpetuate dominance, embedding control into protocols, narratives, and institutions that regulate behavior and suppress resistance without continuous confrontation and violence.

This shift from force to power is not merely tactical but paradigmatic. It represents a refinement in the logic of control, ensuring that dominance is no longer dependent on repeated displays of strength but instead becomes woven into the social fabric itself. Power reconfigures victory into enduring authority, creating an architecture of dominance that shapes the boundaries of what is possible and permissible.

THE LIMITS OF FORCE

Force is the most conspicuous and dramatic expression of dominance. Its logic is straightforward: overwhelm opposition through superior strength and greater violence. Military campaigns, police crackdowns, and acts of physical coercion exemplify the operations of force, asserting control through the direct application of violence.

However, force is inherently limited for three reasons. First, each act of force depletes resources—whether soldiers, money, or political capital—making sustained campaigns unsustainable over time. Second, force resolves immediate conflicts but leaves unresolved tensions, as the defeated retain their capacity and desire to resist. Third, force fails to embed control into enduring systems, requiring renewed confrontation with each challenge, creating a cycle of conflict that undermines stability.

Force, while effective in the moment, is a temporary solution to an enduring problem. It may win battles, but it cannot secure lasting authority.

The Emergence of Power

Power begins where force ends. It emerges not from the act of victory itself but from the systems built in its wake. Power transforms the outcomes of force into rules, norms, and structures that dictate behavior, creating an order in which compliance becomes automatic and resistance appears futile.

Power achieves this transformation through several mechanisms:

Rule Creation: Rules, standards, statistics, and best practices translate the brute outcomes of force into structured authority, embedding dominance into the routines of daily life.

System Building: Institutions and networks enforce these rules, diffusing the burden of control across a broader infrastructure, thereby minimizing the need for direct intervention.

Perception of Inevitability: Power relies on the perception that resistance is futile or unimaginable. By institutionalizing the memory of force's initial victory, power deters future challenges without the need for repeated confrontation.

Expansion of Control: Power grows as allies, bystanders, and even the defeated align themselves with the established system, reinforcing dominance and marginalizing dissent.

Where force compels through its conspicuous

application, power governs through inconspicuous omnipresence, embedding itself in the systems that regulate life and shaping the boundaries of what can be imagined or contested.

Four Forms of Power

In our time—the Age of Global Apartheid and Planetary Ecocide—Empire wields four distinct yet interlocking forms of power: ruling powers, disciplinary powers, normalizing powers, and optimizing powers. The concatenation of these powers forms a dense, self-reinforcing architecture of control that sustains and perpetuates systems of dominance.

Ruling powers assert their dominance through ritualized spectacles designed to glorify the so-called "achievements" of Empire's dominant groups—wealthy white men, their proxies, and their self-fashioned redeemers. These choreographed displays manufacture illusions of superiority and authority, legitimizing domination while entrenching hierarchical power. Tactics of shock and awe—such as military parades and the televised bombings of alleged "terrorist" strongholds—combine overwhelming displays of force with calculated visual grandeur to intimidate dissent, normalize violence, and consolidate the ruling class's control. By presenting power as both inevitable and awe-inspiring, these spectacles sustain the illusion of Empire's invincibility and institutionalize the memory of force's initial victory.

Equally pervasive are the ideological performances embedded in public holidays venerating the supposed benevolence of founding fathers, the hagiographic portrayals of military, political, and corporate leaders in popular media, and the ostentatious pomp surrounding the public appearances of elites. These carefully curated spectacles frame hierarchy as desirable, domination as inevitable, and the concentration of power as virtuous. By cloaking exploitation in the guise of tradition, heroism, and moral order, these spectacles mask the violence of Empire, making its systems of oppression appear righteous and immutable.

DISCIPLINARY POWERS operate through routine examinations that transform the biases of the dominant class into seemingly objective standards and stereotypes. These evaluations categorize and rank individuals, embedding hierarchies into the structures of daily life. Teachers grading students, employers appraising workers, and social workers scrutinizing welfare recipients illustrate how these processes reinforce systemic inequality under the guise of meritocratic assessment. These examinations are deliberately designed to ensure that subordinate groups—particularly the colonized and racialized—

are consistently deemed deficient, internalizing a sense of inadequacy. Meanwhile, dominant groups are routinely affirmed as exemplary, encouraged to see their privilege not as a product of systemic advantage but as evidence of inherent merit.

NORMALIZING POWERS transform the biases embedded in disciplinary systems into seemingly objective statistical "facts." By using biased surveys, they rationalize stereotypes that depict marginalized groups as inherently "inferior." Social scientists and technocrats employ these mechanisms to shape public policy, reframing ideological constructs as technical realities.

Through the aggregation and analysis of data derived from disciplinary processes, normalizing powers "prove" the inadequacy of subordinate groups while affirming the supposed merit of dominant ones. This process objectifies meritocracy, manufacturing legitimacy for hierarchical systems under the guise of impartial analysis.

OPTIMIZING POWERS utilize the statistical "facts" produced by normalizing powers to formulate variable controls and feedback systems that compel marginalized groups to conform to the standards of the ruling class. These powers promote self-regulation, encouraging individuals to internalize systems of domination by framing compliance as a pathway to progress, efficiency, or self-improvement. Social engineers, management consultants, and public relations professionals deploy these mechanisms to shape behavior, reinforcing systemic inequities under the guise of neutrality and advancement.

Optimizing powers present subordinate groups—particularly the colonized and racialized—with a seemingly attainable path to inclusion by emulating the performance of dominant groups or adhering to their dictates. However, this path is an illusion that obscures the structural barriers sustaining exclusion. A key tactic of optimizing powers is the strategic fractioning of "talented tenths" from subordinate groups, empowering these individuals as proxies and redeemers who serve the interests of the dominant groups (the white man, the colonizer). These proxies function to uphold and legitimize the existing hierarchy while reinforcing the very systems of power that maintain their group's subordination.

The Architecture of Domination

The interplay between these four forms of power creates a deeply entrenched and self-sustaining architecture of domination.

Ruling powers construct spectacles that exalt hierarchy. *Disciplinary powers* embed these hierarchies into daily routines and practices. *Normalizing powers* reframe these hierarchies as objective truths. *Optimizing powers* compel compliance with these truths, making domination appear natural and inevitable.

This architecture is insidious, drawing its strength from its inconspicuousness and omnipresence. It masquerades as neutral, necessary, and virtuous, masking its reliance on coercion and exploitation. However, when its foundations are exposed, its fragility becomes apparent. Resistance requires not only opposing the conspicuous forces of domination but also dismantling the inconspicuous systems that sustain them.

By exposing the mechanisms of ruling, disciplinary, normalizing, and optimizing powers, we can begin to unravel the logics that perpetuate dominance, creating space for alternative systems rooted in autonomy, care, and confluence.

The Dangers We Face

Those who seek to expose and resist the mechanisms of power inevitably face a sophisticated matrix of violence—physical, cultural, institutional, carceral, and behavioral. Empire's architecture of domination is designed to suppress dissent and enforce compliance, deploying coercive tactics that target both individuals and communities to maintain the status quo. Each form of violence functions not in isolation but as part of an interlocking system, ensuring that resistance is met with layered and often inconspicuous forms of repression.

"Guns and Bombs" – Physical Violence

Empire's most immediate and visible response to rebellion is brute force, physical violence. This includes the militarized policing of domestic unrest, the bombing of communities labeled as threats, and the targeting of activists through direct confrontation. Physical violence serves not only to threaten and brutalize rebels but also to destroy the material and symbolic spaces where rebellion takes root—be it neighborhoods, protest camps, or autonomous zones.

Militarized force functions as a spectacle as much as a weapon—an overt display of ruling power. Heavily armed police, drones overhead, and live-streamed military strikes on "terrorist" enclaves send clear messages to those who might resist: the full force of Empire will descend upon those who dare to challenge it. This violence enforces fear, silences dissent, and reinforces Empire's monopoly on the means of destruction.

"Smoke and Mirrors" – Cultural Violence

Cultural violence operates in more subtle but equally insidious ways. Empire obscures historical realities, mystifies the conditions of oppression, and distorts narratives to delegitimize resistance. Through propaganda, media, education, and cultural production, it erases histories of rebellion and resistance while promoting myths that sustain its hegemony.

This violence often disguises itself as enlightenment or entertainment—functioning as disciplinary power in one guise and ruling power in another. Textbooks erase anti-colonial struggles, films depict rebels as chaotic threats to order, and media narratives portray activists as irrational or extremist. Through its cultural machinery, Empire manufactures a false consensus in which systemic domination is normalized, rebellion is rendered futile, and resistance is framed as dangerous or delusional.

By controlling the stories a society tells about itself, cultural violence normalizes oppression and delegitimizes alternatives, ensuring that Empire's worldview becomes the only conceivable reality.

"Policies and Procedures" – Institutional Violence

Institutional violence is deployed through bureaucratic systems that surveil, regulate, and constrain lives under the guise of neutrality. These systems create and enforce policies designed to monitor and suppress potential rebels, often targeting them through mechanisms that appear impartial or necessary.

From zoning laws that dismantle protest spaces to immigration policies that marginalize dissenting communities, institutional violence polices livelihoods in insidious ways. Surveillance technologies track movements, monitor communications, and compile databases of suspected agitators. Licensing requirements, audits, and "risk assessments" become tools to suffocate grassroots organizing and resistance efforts.

Institutional violence weaves together disciplinary, normalizing, and optimizing powers, cloaking itself in the guise of order and efficiency. It renders its victims invisible, framing repression as an inevitable and regrettable necessity of governance. Its strength lies in its inconspicuousness, disqualifying dissenters before they can openly resist, ensuring domination without the need for spectacle.

"Prisons and Fortresses" – Carceral Violence

Carceral violence directly confines and excludes those who resist Empire's systems. From mass incarceration to detention centers and fortified borders, these structures are designed to contain rebellion, both physically and symbolically.

Prisons and detention centers incapacitate individuals who challenge the system, isolating them from their communities and forcing them into regimes of control and surveillance. Border walls and immigration detention facilities ensure that vulnerable populations remain out of sight and excluded from access to resources and autonomy.

Carceral systems exemplify disciplinary powers by reinforcing the divisions of Global Apartheid, segregating populations along lines of race, class, and nationality. Simultaneously operating as ruling powers, these structures do more than confine rebels—they broadcast a chilling message to all: the cost of dissent is confinement, exclusion, and erasure.

"Carrots and Sticks" – Behavioral Violence

Behavioral violence works through incentives and punishments to manipulate individuals and foster compliance with Empire's agenda. Unlike physical or carceral violence, this form of repression reshapes behavior through more subtle forms of coercion, aligning actions with the interests of the ruling class.

Examples include surveillance-based reward systems that promote conformity—such as social credit scores or workplace monitoring tools—and punitive measures like fines, demotions, or public shaming for those who deviate from prescribed norms. Integrating ruling, disciplinary, normalizing, and optimizing powers, these mechanisms present themselves as instruments of efficiency, self-improvement, or progress, rendering compliance seemingly rational while obscuring their coercive foundations.

Behavioral violence discourages rebellion by fostering complicity, creating the illusion that one's best option is to play within the rules of the system rather than oppose it. Over time, individuals internalize domination, policing themselves and each other in ways that serve Empire's goals.

LIBERATION

The fugitive planners in the opening story teach us that true liberation lies not in opposing the force of Empire directly, but in dismantling the systems of power that sustain its dominance. Force may be met with resistance in the moment, but enduring freedom requires challenging the structures that normalize oppression, the narratives that legitimize inequality, and the mechanisms that compel compliance.

Liberation begins with exposure. The mechanisms of rule, discipline, normalization, and optimization must be laid bare, their inconspicuous operations rendered starkly to those who live under their weight. This exposure disrupts the myths of inevitability that sustain Empire's control, revealing that its power is neither natural nor immutable.

Dismantling these mechanisms requires more than critique; it demands the creation of alternatives. Fugitive planners remind us that care, confluence, and collective flourishing are not merely values but practices—ways of building communities that prioritize relational autonomy and mutual support over hierarchy and exploitation. Resistance thus becomes an act of world-making, imagining and enacting infrastructures where life thrives beyond Empire's logic of domination.

However, such resistance does not come without risks. As we have seen, Empire's response to dissent is multifaceted, employing physical, cultural, institutional, carceral, and behavioral violence to suppress rebellion and enforce compliance. This violence seeks to isolate and intimidate, to render resistance futile by making it appear dangerous, disorganized, or impossible. Yet, as the maroons demonstrated, even the most entrenched systems of domination are vulnerable to disruption.

Confronting Our Traumas

Global apartheid persists not because it is inevitable or inexplicable, but because it is sustained by systems of domination that thrive on division and indifference. These systems fracture human lives through violence and neglect, weaponizing trauma to maintain control. The colonizer, traumatized into callousness, is conditioned to dominate and disregard. The colonized, traumatized into submission, is conditioned to accept domination, or navigate it through exclusionary strategies. Both are ensnared in intergenerational cycles of harm that perpetuate global apartheid.

Let us consider two figures—the white boy who witnesses racial violence, and the Black girl whose father is killed by that violence—to examine how trauma distorts care, sustains these systems, and might be confronted and healed.

THE WHITE BOY
Callousness, Saviorism, and Re-Enactment

Consider a young white boy taken by his father to witness a lynching. He sees the brutalized body of a Black man, hears the celebratory crowd, and feels a flicker of horror. His father reassures him, "We are protecting our way of life." The boy's fear and confusion are silenced by the paternal voice of authority, teaching him to suppress his discomfort and rationalize the violence.

A modern parallel might involve a white boy watching the video of George Floyd's murder. He feels horror and outrage, but is quickly inundated with competing narratives: "He was resisting arrest." "This isn't about race." "It's a tragedy, but what can we do?" In both cases, the boy's initial response of care is disrupted by rationalizations that distort his perception of harm and injustice.

As the boy matures, his unresolved trauma shapes his relationship to the world in deeply consequential ways. He might internalize the rationalizations he was taught, numbing himself to Black suffering and dismissing systemic injustice as irrelevant to his life. Conditioned by the narratives of his upbringing, he may come to see such harm as inevitable or even justified, growing callous and indifferent to the violence that surrounds him.

Alternatively, his trauma might compel him toward a different response, one of intervention—but on terms that reaffirm his centrality. Adopting the role of a white savior, he seeks to act on the care he could not express as a child. Yet, this saviorism, while outwardly righteous, is fundamentally rooted in his own unresolved wounds. Like a Bruce Wayne or Batman figure, his attempts to address harm become a means of soothing his guilt and reclaiming his sense of moral integrity. In striving to be the hero of the story, he recenters his agency, relegating Black autonomy and resistance to the background of his benevolence. His care, distorted by trauma, serves to perpetuate the very hierarchies he seeks to transcend.

In many instances, this unresolved trauma takes a darker turn. Internalizing the violence he once witnessed, the white boy might reenact it to assert power and mask the insecurities born of his earlier passivity. Unable to confront the cruelty he observed and the complicity he inherited, he channels his fear and confusion into acts that replicate the very harm he initially recoiled from.

Whether his response takes the form of callousness, saviorism, or reenactment, the underlying pattern remains the same: his trauma prevents him from confronting the structural forces that sustain racial violence. Instead of dismantling these systems, he becomes ensnared in their logic, reproducing the cycles of domination that perpetuate harm. His inability to resolve his own relationship to care and accountability leaves him trapped, both a product of these systems and an unwitting agent of their continuation.

THE BLACK GIRL
From Inferiority to Exclusionary Excellence

Now consider a young Black girl whose father is killed by police. She grows up hearing how he begged for his life, how his killers faced no consequences, and how the world seemed to move on. Her trauma is not just the loss of her father, but the collective grief and powerlessness her community carries.

She learns that her survival depends on navigating a world hostile to her existence. Her trauma may manifest as internalized inferiority, where she accepts her community's dehumanization as inevitable. But if she resists this narrative, she may strive to embody "Black excellence," seeking to escape vulnerability by proving her worth to a world that denies it.

As an adult, she may ascend to prominence within the "talented tenth," using her success to distance herself from the conditions that shaped her father's death. Over time, she may come to view the vulnerability of ordinary Black men, like her father, as a failure to "adapt"—a fragility she cannot afford to acknowledge. If she becomes a high-powered public prosecutor, for example, this perception might drive her to enforce harsher measures against Black men, channeling her unresolved trauma into punitive actions.

This distortion of care transforms her success into a tool of exclusion. Her drive to escape the dehumanizing forces that shaped her father's death becomes entangled with the need to prove herself exceptional. In doing so, she risks aligning with the very systems that perpetuated the violence she seeks to resist. While her achievements may be celebrated, they often reinforce hierarchies that isolate her from her community and uphold the logics of domination.

Rather than dismantling the structures that dehumanized her father, she becomes consumed by the need to transcend them on their terms. This pursuit, framed as liberation, ties her aspirations to systems that reward individual distinction at the expense of collective care, ultimately reproducing the isolation and fragmentation her trauma imposed.

Trauma as a Mechanism of Division

The experiences of the white boy and the Black girl illustrate how trauma sustains systems of domination by distorting care. These systems harm individuals and condition entire populations to rationalize and reproduce harm. Both experiences are fractured, their relationships to care distorted by systems that thrive on division.

These distortions are deliberate, embedded in the operations of imperialist white-supremacist capitalist patriarchy. By subjecting different groups to distinct traumas, these systems fragment and stratify care, making it conditional and selective. The white boy turned savior performs self-righteous acts of care only for those he deems as deserving, while the Black girl turned prosecutor limits her care to those who conform to the anti-Black standards of excellence she has internalized. Both are alienated from the relational, spontaneous care capable of disrupting and challenging these systems of domination.

Confronting Trauma, Reclaiming Care

Freudian psychoanalysis offers a starting point for addressing trauma:

First, recognize that rationalizations for not caring about one's complicity in or acquiescence to genocide, ethnocide, and ecocide are symptoms of unresolved trauma.

Second, uncover the repressed traumatic experiences that inhibit spontaneous acts of care.

This approach helps individuals confront the origins of their anxieties, but does not go far enough.

Building on Frantz Fanon, we must add a third step: situate personal trauma within the broader power formations that produce and exploit it. The white boy must ask: "How was my trauma manipulated to align me with systems of domination?" The Black girl must ask: "How was my trauma manipulated to isolate me from my community?" By connecting personal experiences to systemic structures, both can begin to dismantle the ideologies that distort their care.

But healing demands more than introspection; it requires a radical, embodied practice of care to mend the fractures wrought by trauma. The white boy must transcend saviorism, recognizing that care is not about fixing others but cultivating community with others through embodied practices of recognition, recollection, resistance, and repair. The Black girl must move beyond the confines of exclusionary excellence, embracing embodied forms of care that affirm the dignity, agency, and resilience of her community. Together, they must confront the systems that have shaped their traumas, rejecting the hierarchies that perpetuate human division and suffering.

Yet, this shared endeavor can only proceed if both parties acknowledge a fundamental truth: the trauma of the colonized and oppressed must take precedence. Their agency must be restored first for any collective healing or collaboration to be meaningful. Without this foundational reparation, "working together" risks perpetuating the very systems of domination that healing seeks to dismantle. Furthermore, it is not the responsibility of the colonized and oppressed to address the traumas that colonizers and oppressors inflict upon themselves and their kin—traumas rooted in the pursuit and maintenance of advantage within oppressive systems. Instead, colonizers and oppressors bear responsibility for the traumas they have inflicted—both directly and indirectly—on the colonized and oppressed as a result of colonization and systemic domination. This asymmetry of responsibility reflects the profound asymmetry of power and harm embedded in such systems.

CULTIVATING CREATIVE MALADJUSTMENT

Global apartheid persists because systems of domination thrive on division, indifference, and distorted care. These systems condition individuals to uphold hierarchies of power, rewarding those who conform to their logic. The white boy who becomes indifferent or assumes the mantle of a savior, and the Black girl who becomes submissive or exclusionary, are often celebrated as "well-adjusted" to the world as it is. Yet their responses—whether marked by callousness, saviorism, submission, or exclusionary ambition—are not signs of health, but symptoms of complicity in harm.

As Martin Luther King Jr. reminds us:

> There are some things in our nation and in the world to which I'm proud to be maladjusted, and which I call upon all men of good will to remain maladjusted until the good society is realized. I must honestly say that I never intend to adjust myself to segregation and discrimination. I never intend to become adjusted to religious bigotry. I never intend to adjust myself to economic conditions which take necessities from the many to give luxuries to the few. I never intend to adjust myself to the madness of militarism and the self-defeating effects of physical violence.

If you or those around you find yourselves "well-adjusted" to life within the genocidal, ethnocidal, and ecocidal machinery of Empire—indifferent to the atrocities of global apartheid and its pervasive violences—it is worth examining how systemic traumatization has conditioned this submission. Beyond the immediate harms of toxic relationships and environments shaped by colonial legacies and racialized rule, we must confront the relentless flood of live-streamed genocides, viral videos of police killings, reports of mass shootings, the trivialization of colonization and slavery in historical narratives, and the glorification of violence in media and entertainment. These mechanisms do not merely (mis)educate or entertain; they subtly condition indifference, eroding collective care, deepening helplessness, and normalizing violence as an inevitable and inescapable reality.

To embrace (re-)creative maladjustment is to reject alignment with systems of domination. It is to resist narratives that justify fractured care, to interrogate the roots of trauma, to reclaim the relational, collective capacity to care, and to envision a world beyond these systems of domination. The white boy and the Black girl, if creatively maladjusted, might refuse the roles imposed on them—he, by standing in common cause with those his society has dehumanized; she, by honoring and uplifting the struggles of her community. Together, they could begin to dismantle the systems that distorted their care, fostering relationships rooted in practices of recognition, recollection, resistance, and repair.

Creative maladjustment is not merely a refusal to comply; it is an active commitment to recognition, recollection, resistance, and repair. It requires the courage to question the rationalization and narrativization of traumatic experiences that fracture care and uphold domination.

Rape & Femicide
The Foundations of Empire's Power

Rape and femicide as means of inflicting trauma are not incidental to the functioning of Empire—they are foundational. These acts are public assertions of power, instruments of domination that serve to enforce submission and terrorize communities into compliance. By targeting women, Empire severs relational bonds, fractures communities, and distorts care. This violence is not merely physical; it is also systemic and communicative, a language of control designed to perpetuate the hierarchies upon which Empire depends.

The Historical Roots of Femicide

Empire's reliance on femicide can be traced to the rise of patriarchal systems, predating the global structures of domination we recognize today. Women, especially those who were carriers of ancestral knowledge, were deliberately targeted. Healers, midwives, and spiritual leaders—often branded as witches—were among the first victims, as their roles sustained networks of care that challenged the consolidation of power. Rape and femicide became primary tools to dismantle these networks, erasing the relational systems women embodied and asserting control through violence and annihilation.

Rape and femicide have been adapted to meet Empire's changing needs. With the onset of colonization, femicide became a central mechanism of imperial expansion. Conquest was not limited to the seizing of land and resources; it was also an assault on relational systems that resisted imperial domination. The sexual violence inflicted on Indigenous and African women during colonization was not incidental. It served to terrorize communities, sever kinship bonds, and render resistance futile. By targeting women, colonizers struck at the heart of relational life, ensuring that patriarchal and imperial hierarchies could take root.

Femicide and the Logic of Empire

As Empire evolved, so too did the role of femicide within its machinery of domination. In the industrial phase of capitalism, femicide was deeply entwined with the exploitation of women's labor. Women, particularly racialized women, were drawn into factories and plantations, their lives marked by disposability. The constant threat of violence served to enforce compliance and instill fear. Femicide was not merely a product of exploitation—it was an essential mechanism for maintaining control over vulnerable laboring populations.

Today, in the age of logistical capitalism, rape and femicide have shifted to the border zones, offshored manufacturing plants, and migration corridors that sustain global supply chains. Women working in sweatshops, traveling along migratory routes, or confined to refugee camps are exposed to femicidal violence as a systemic practice. These acts communicate a stark message: women of the lower classes, particularly racialized women, are deemed expendable within Empire's economic and political order. These acts fracture communities and instill fear, undermining the solidarity needed to resist the exploitative systems governing these spaces.

The Communicative Power of Rape and Femicide

Rape and femicide are not isolated acts of violence; they are deliberate, systemic tools of control. As Segato argues, these acts communicate dominance, inscribing power onto bodies and communities. Their primary function is to generate trauma that fractures relationships, distorts care, and undermines collective resistance.

This violence reinforces hierarchies of race and class by dictating which lives are valued and which are dismissed. The rape and murder of a poor Black African woman—whether working in a sweatshop, traveling a migrant route, or living in a refugee camp—are often trivialized, her suffering rendered routine and forgettable by systems that devalue her existence. In contrast, the rape of a white woman in a professional or domestic setting is sensationalized, framed as a shocking violation of societal norms. Yet even affluent white women may remain silent about their assaults, fearing that disclosure will invite public scrutiny and mark them with the vulnerability typically assigned to marginalized women. This fear is heightened to the degree that any aspect of their life may be perceived as transgressing the standards of propriety, purity, and morality expected of their race, class ambitions, or professional aspirations. These dynamics underscore how sexual violence both enforces domination and reinforces hierarchies of worth and disposability.

The power of rape and femicide lies in their ability to produce trauma that isolates survivors, instills fear in communities, and fragments relational bonds. Trauma reshapes care into a conditional, survival-driven act, corroding the solidarity and mutual support necessary to resist oppression. Survivors are silenced, communities are fractured, and compliance with systems of domination is reinforced.

Moreover, this violence perpetuates cycles of harm. Men of lower classes and "lesser" races, "emasculated" by systems of oppression, are conditioned to reclaim their masculinity by reenacting the sexual violence historically imposed upon their female counterparts—perpetuating harm with the limited means available to them. Some resist this conditioning but adopt a patriarchal saviorism, akin to white saviorism, in an effort to "protect" women from rape and femicide. While appearing well-intentioned, this posture centers male agency and unresolved wounds, sidelining female autonomy and resistance in favor of patriarchal acts of benevolence. Distorted by trauma, the patriarchal saviorism adopted by men of marginalized races and classes inadvertently reinforces the hierarchies they seek to dismantle. By confining, disempowering, and demanding conformity from women in the name of protecting them, patriarchal saviors sustain systems of control rather than fostering genuine liberation.

By distorting care and weakening relational bonds, rape and femicide ensure the preservation of Empire's hierarchies. Their violence does not simply harm individuals; it undermines the very connections and practices that could challenge oppressive systems. Empire's evolution underscores rape and femicide as enduring and adaptable mechanisms of control, designed to sever relational bonds and enforce submission across shifting contexts.

RECLAIMING CARE AND RELATIONALITY

Rape and femicide derive their power from distorting care and severing relational bonds. To resist this violence, communities must reclaim care as an act of collective resistance. This begins with recognition: naming rape and femicide not as isolated events, but as systemic tools of control designed to dismantle communal ties. By understanding their role in fracturing relationships, we can take the first steps toward restoring the connections they seek to destroy.

Transformation means reshaping care into a relational and embodied practice that rejects Empire's logic of division. Through embodied practices of recognition, recollection, resistance, and repair, communities can dismantle the structures that sustain sexual violence and rebuild systems of care capable of confronting and undoing its power.

Reclaiming care also requires rejecting the fragmented and conditional narratives imposed by trauma. Instead, it calls for cultivating communities that actively challenge Empire's reliance on rape and femicide to uphold its hierarchies, fostering relational practices that resist domination and affirm collective resilience.

Conclusion:
Empire's Next Moves &
Maroon Countermeasures

Throughout this book, we have argued that Empire is not a monolithic institution but an assemblage of abstract and concrete machines—some co-opted from pre-colonial social formations, others with distinctly imperial and colonial origins, and still others emerging from decolonial and counter-colonial resistance, only to be captured and perverted into neo-colonial apparatuses. Its continuity depends on the relentless recomposition of these machinic assemblages, adjusting their configurations to absorb crises, neutralize threats, and sustain the dual fracture that underwrites its domination: the fracture that constructs superior and inferior races of man, entrenching Global Apartheid, and the fracture that positions mankind as separate from—and in dominion over—its environment, driving Planetary Ecocide.

Dismantling Empire requires sabotaging and short-circuiting the connections that sustain its machinery, disrupting its operations until the system collapses under its own disarticulation. Yet dismantling alone is insufficient, for too many of us remain entangled in its infrastructures of survival. Alongside disassembly, we must construct alternative life-support systems— assemblages of sustenance, relation, and regeneration—that enable us to endure and thrive amid the ruination of Empire.

This demands not only the reclamation and repair of pre-colonial, decolonial, and counter-colonial machines—those wrested from Empire's grasp, salvaged from the wreckage it leaves in its wake, or hidden in fugitive refuges beyond its reach—but also the strategic co-optation of imperial and colonial machines, repurposing them to subvert Empire's genocidal, ethnocidal, and ecocidal logics. At the same time, it requires the invention of new decolonial and counter-colonial machines that connect and coordinate all of the above, forming insurgent, maroon infrastructures capable of sustaining diverse struggles for liberation.

To do so, we must interrogate the vulnerabilities within our own pre-colonial, decolonial, and counter-colonial machines—what weaknesses allowed Empire to co-opt, displace, or destroy them? What faults made them susceptible to capture? At the same time, we must analyze Empire's machinery: how its ruling powers consolidate authority, how its disciplinary powers regulate bodies, how its normalizing powers manufacture consent, and how its optimizing powers extract and exploit at scale. Our aim is to turn the tables on Empire—to co-opt, displace, and dismantle its apparatuses just as it has done to ours.

This requires tracing how Empire's machines determine population demographics, enforce separation through geographic bordering regimes, and arrest peoples and places within progressive stages of historiographic development. It means recognizing the layered forms of violence—physical, cultural, institutional, carceral, and behavioral—that sustain these operations and mapping their interrelations so we may skillfully counteract them.

Empire's machinery operates across multiple scales: sub-molecular, molecular, and molar. The sub-molecular scale is that of the flesh—how Empire weaponizes our own organs against us, conditioning our senses and our brain chemistry to shape perception, desire, and reaction. The molecular scale is that of social bonds—how Empire exploits our relationships, threatening the ties between parents and children, friends, lovers, and co-workers, using fear, dependency, and coercion to enforce conformity. The molar scale is that of populations—how Empire deploys statistics to classify, predict, and manage risk, optimizing the times, places, and bodies upon which it unleashes violence for maximum effect.

At each scale, we must counter Empire's machinic assemblages. On the sub-molecular scale, how do we deprogram our senses and recalibrate our brain chemistry—shifting the vibe, intensifying our desire for resistance, sharpening our perception of opportunities to defy Empire, and fortifying the courage to seize them? On the molecular scale, how do we form rebellious packs, cultivating relationships sustained by insubordination rather than conformity? On the molar scale, how do we generate noise so that Empire cannot extract the signals it needs to determine risk—disrupting its ability to predict which times, places, and bodies are most critical to target?

To break Empire's circuits, we must disrupt its ability to perceive, predict, and control—faulting its logics at every level until the system crashes under the weight of its own failures. Yet dismantling Empire's machinery is only half the work. At each scale, we must also construct alternative life-support systems that sustain and strengthen us against Empire's violence. At the sub-molecular scale, this means nourishing and protecting our bodies—learning to care for and defend them against the elements. At the molecular scale, it means fostering tonic rather than toxic relations—forming bonds sustained by care rather than coercion or conformity. At the molar scale, it requires reconfiguring how we distribute resources and responsibilities—spreading vulnerabilities across our networks so that no single individual or group can be easily singled out as a weak link or vital node to capture and exploit.

And survival is not enough. We must learn to thrive in ways that Empire cannot capture—sustaining ourselves and one another while rendering Empire increasingly incapable of sustaining itself.

Empire's Next Moves

Empire is currently consolidating its grip over emerging fractures in its system, adapting to crises of legitimacy and resource depletion. Drawing on its historical resilience, Empire's strategies focus on fortifying its machinery of domination. These include intensifying surveillance capitalism, expanding its planetary technosphere, and integrating new hegemonic players like China into its overarching logic of control. Key areas where Empire is poised to act are outlined below, followed by a framework to begin developing maroon countermeasures designed to resist these strategies.

Refinement of Surveillance Capitalism

Empire is advancing toward a deeper integration of human behavior, affect, and desire into its machinery of control. Surveillance capitalism intensifies, embedding itself within the most intimate, molecular and submolecular dimensions of life to appropriate and externalize the costs of social reproduction. Through AI, biometric surveillance, algorithmic governance, and the pervasive pornoscopic logic of social media, Empire commodifies attention, emotions, and desires as instruments of extraction and domination. Exploiting intimacy as a site of profit and regulation, it enlists individuals in their own surveillance and subjugation. Autonomy is systematically eroded as aspirations, relationships, and ways of being are recalibrated to serve the imperatives of capital accumulation.

This refinement of surveillance capitalism hinges on normalizing digital ecologies that integrate augmented reality, virtual spaces, and algorithmic decision-making into everyday life. On the molar scale, this "metaverse" will serve as a platform for behavioral optimization and commodification, distracting populations from material exploitation while deepening their integration into systems of control. These digital infrastructures will reinforce hierarchies by gatekeeping access to resources, visibility, and power.

FORTIFICATION OF THE TECHNOSPHERE

Empire is amplifying its planetary infrastructure of control, leveraging speculative technologies to tighten its grasp over material and ecological systems.

Under the guise of progress and security, it advances "solutions" to the crises of the Anthropocene that, in reality, extend the reach and intensify the grip of its technosphere over the planet. Empire's planners assure us that geoengineering projects, carbon capture schemes, and renewable technologies—manufactured from vast quantities of rare earth metals extracted from the lands of denigrated races of humanity—will guarantee "sustainability." In truth, these developments facilitate the "managed depletion" of Earth's resources, accelerating planetary ecocide while maximizing elite pleasures and profits.

Concurrently, Empire's military-industrial machine is undergoing reconfiguration. AI weapons, autonomous drones, and surveillance platforms are being woven into an ever-expanding architecture of war. These techno-military systems do not merely serve defense; they function as Empire's means of recalibration, adapting to crises by amplifying violence, justifying new modes of control, and reformatting global hierarchies of extraction and accumulation.

Reconfiguration of Multipolar Hegemony

The shifting balance of power, particularly the rise of China and the BRICS nations, does not signal Empire's decline but yet another recalibration. Empire is not wedded to a singular hegemon; its machinic logic operates through modularity, integrating emerging powers into its circuits of racial capitalism and ecological extraction. The rivalry between hegemonic blocs (e.g., NATO vs. BRICS) will be cast as a geopolitical and ideological contest, yet beneath the spectacle, their shared commitments to extraction, domination, and ecological devastation persist.

This competition will unfold through both hot and cold wars, but war itself is not an anathema to Empire—it is a fundamental mechanism of its self-replication. War functions as Empire's recalibration device, driving technological innovation, restructuring global economies, and justifying ever-expanding mechanisms of control. These conflicts are not ruptures in the system but programmed accelerations, ensuring that destruction and reconstruction remain key engines of imperial sustainability.

Expansion of the Carceral State

As fractures widen and resistance intensifies, Empire will expand its carceral systems, transforming entire populations into captives of its machinery. Border fortifications, biometric tracking, predictive policing, and militarized protest suppression will serve as instruments of mass pacification. Prisons and detention centers, already laboratories of racialized control and sites of sexual violence, will be further optimized to experiment with new methods of containment and compliance. As Empire's crisis-management machine recalibrates, any movement threatening systemic transformation will be neutralized through both overt repression and algorithmic modulation of dissent.

Exploitation of Crisis Narratives

Empire will weaponize crises—climate disasters, pandemics, economic instability—as opportunities to consolidate control. These emergencies will justify emergency measures that erode rights, expand surveillance, and reinforce systemic dependencies. Framed as necessary for public safety, sustainability, or economic recovery, these measures will obscure their true function: reinforcing the circuits of extraction, enclosure, and hierarchical domination. The increasing precarity of life under Empire will be exploited to normalize compliance, presenting Empire's machinery as the only viable solution to escalating crises.

Suppression of TEK and Resistance Movements

Empire will intensify its suppression of Transformative Ecological Knowledge (TEK) and grassroots resistance movements, seeking to erase, criminalize, or appropriate practices that threaten its machinery. TEK, embodying practices of ecological care and regeneration, will be dismissed as archaic, reduced to spectacle, or plundered for corporate gain. Simultaneously, Indigenous and Maroon sovereignty movements will be met with heightened repression, as their frameworks pose direct threats to Empire's logic of extraction and control.

Maroon Countermeasures

To confront Empire's escalating strategies of domination, maroon countermeasures must expand in both scope and scale, adapting alongside its machinic recalibrations. Rooted in the enduring traditions of marronage—practices of escape, refusal, and (re-)creation incubated within the Black radical tradition—these countermeasures do not merely resist but actively disrupt, reconfigure, and exceed Empire's machinery of control. They must operate as an insurgent system that intercepts, subverts, and transforms Empire's attempts at self-repair into points of cascading failure.

Maroon countermeasures operate across a spectrum of resistance and transformation, fracturing Empire's machinic coherence while generating autonomous formations capable of sustaining alternative worlds.

PETIT MARRONAGE: Dispersed, everyday acts of defiance that erode Empire's control at the molecular and sub-molecular sclae. By reclaiming stolen time, cultivating autonomous zones, and subverting predictive surveillance, petit marronage manifests as vibe shifts, pack formations, and fugitive practices that corrode Empire's ability to perceive, predict, and neutralize dissent. These subtle yet essential fractures create pockets of autonomy, care, and relational resilience within Empire's cybernetic enclosures, ensuring its apparatus remains unable to fully optimize itself.

GRAND MARRONAGE: Radical ruptures that sever connection to Empire's molar scale infrastructure entirely. Historically, grand marronage took the form of maroon societies, fugitive networks, and the refusal of subjugation through self-exile. Today, grand marronage manifests in mass defections from Empire's machinic order—economic disobedience, digital and physical exodus, infrastructural sabotage, and coordinated insurrections that dismantle Empire's operational integrity.

These modes of marronage are deeply interwoven. The persistence of petit marronage weakens Empire's predictive capacities and softens the terrain for larger ruptures, while grand marronage catalyzes and amplifies everyday refusals, ensuring that insurrectionary potential remains an active force within Empire's fractures.

Maroon countermeasures must operate across the sub-molecular, molecular, and molar scales, strategically targeting Empire's machinic assemblages at each level.

SHIFTING VIBES: At the sub-molecular scale, countermeasures disrupt the sensory conditioning and affective modulations that sustain compliance. By hacking perception, reorienting desire, and altering the neural rhythms that Empire weaponizes, we weaken the internalized circuits of control. Guerrilla media, sonic sabotage, and algorithmic disobedience become methods of breaking the coherence of Empire's machinic gaze.

FORMING PACKS: At the molecular scale, countermeasures build networks of relational insubordination. Empire sustains itself by infiltrating and regulating social bonds, deploying coercion to enforce machinic cohesion. Counter-machinic packs operate through relational autonomy—networks of fugitivity, mutual aid formations, and insurgent kinships that operate outside Empire's predictive mechanisms.

MOVING MASSES: At the molar scale, countermeasures align dispersed acts of resistance into collective intensifications. General strikes, land reclamations, digital exodus campaigns, and mass uprisings channel molecular and sub-molecular disruptions into movements capable of breaking Empire's strategic architectures of control. These moments are not spontaneous ruptures but the culmination of interwoven maroon infrastructures, operating in sync to transform Empire's fractures into points of irreversible systemic failure.

Maroon countermeasures must not only resist but actively convert Empire's machinic weaknesses into sites of insurgency. Empire's next moves—its refinement of surveillance capitalism, its fortification of the technosphere, its reconfiguration of multipolar hegemony, its expansion of the carceral state, its exploitation of crisis narratives, and its suppression of TEK and resistance movements—must be met with counter-machinic strategies that invert their intended functions.

How do we scramble Empire's data networks, turning its predictive analytics into a liability rather than an advantage?

How do we undermine its technological enclosures, forcing its infrastructures to work against its own extractive logic?

How do we mobilize autonomous packs and insurgent confluences that evade surveillance while escalating resistance?

How do we sever Empire's ability to metabolize crisis, ensuring its next rupture is beyond repair?

Maroon countermeasures must operate as an emergent system of refusal, sabotage, and regenerative world-building. The goal is not only to survive but to render Empire's apparatuses unsustainable—

to accelerate its unraveling while constructing parallel structures that sustain fugitive life beyond its grasp.

Through this interplay of disruption and re-creation, marronage becomes more than resistance; it becomes the mechanism through which Empire's machinic order is rendered obsolete. Our task is not merely to flee, but to fracture, reconfigure, and out-maneuver—to build counter-machines that both dismantle and surpass Empire's capacity for control.

www.ingramcontent.com/pod-product-compliance
Lightning Source LLC
LaVergne TN
LVHW092050060526
838201LV00047B/1319